Exchange Server 5.5

Accelerated MCSE Study Guide

Exchange Server 5.5

Exam 70–081

Mitch Tulloch, MCSE, MCT

McGraw-Hill
New York   San Francisco   Washington, D.C.   Auckland
Bogotá   Caracas   Lisbon   London   Madrid   Mexico City
Milan   Montreal   New Delhi   San Juan   Singapore
Sydney   Tokyo   Toronto

Library of Congress Cataloging-in Publication

Tulloch, Mitch.
    Accelerated MCSE study guide.   Exhange Server 5.5 / Mitch
Tulloch.
        p.   cm.
    "Exam 70-081."
    ISBN 0–07–134771-2
    1. Electronic data processing personnel—Certification.
    2. Microsoft software—Examinations Study guides. 3. Microsoft
Exchange server. I. Title.
QA76.3.T84 1999
0057'13769—dc21   99-12467
                                            CIP

McGraw-Hill

*A Division of The **McGraw·Hill** Companies*

1 2 3 4 4 6 7 8 9 0 AGM/AGM 9 0 4 3 2 1 0 9

ISBN 0-07-134771-2

Throughout this book, trademarked names are used. Rather than put a trademark
symbol after every occurrence of a trademarked name, we use names in an editorial fashion only, and to the benefit of the trademark owner, with no intention of
infringement of the trademark. Where such designations appear in this book,
they have been printed with initial caps.

Printed and bound by Quebecor Martinsburg.

The sponsoring editor for this book was Michael Sprague, the editing supervisor
was Ruth W. Mannino, and the production supervisor was Clare Stanley. It was set
in Stone Serif by Priscilla Beer of McGraw-Hill's Professional Book Group composi-
tion unit in cooperation with Spring Point Publishing Services.

 This book is printed on recycled, acid-free paper containing a minimum
of 50% recycled de-inked fiber.

Contents

Acknowledgments   ix

Chapter 1   Introduction to This Study Guide   1

Plan Your MCSE Process   1
Prepare for Each Exam   22
Pass One Exam at a Time   29
Focus of This Book: Exam 70-081: Implementing
   and Supporting Microsoft Exchange Server 5.5   43

Chapter 2   Planning and Implementation   45

What Is Exchange Server?   45
Supported Features and Protocols   46
How Does Exchange Server Work?   47
Basic Concepts and Terminology   48
Planning an Exchange Implementation   51
Client Access Licenses   56
Installing Exchange Server   57
Where Do We Go from Here?   60
For Review   60

Chapter 3   Exchange Administrator   63

Exchange Tools   63
The Exchange Administrator Program   65
Permissions and Roles   70
Where Do We Go from Here?   74
For Review   74

Chapter 4   Site   75

Site-Level Directory Objects   75
Site Configuration Container   78
DS Site Configuration   79
Information Store Site Configuration   81
MTA Site Configuration   83

Site Addressing   85
Directory Replication Connector   87
Where Do We Go from Here?   89
For Review   89

Chapter 5   Servers   **93**

Server-Level Directory Objects   93
Servers and Server Containers   96
Message Transfer Agent   99
Directory Service   101
Private Information Store   102
Public Information Store   104
System Attendant   105
Where Do We Go from Here?   106
For Review   107

Chapter 6   Recipients   **109**

Recipients Containers   109
Mailbox   113
Distribution List   116
Custom Recipient   118
Public Folder   120
Mailbox Agent   120
Where Do We Go from Here?   120
For Review   121

Chapter 7   Public Folders   **127**

Creating Public Folders   127
Public Folder Properties   130
Public Folder Permissions   132
Public Folder Replicas   134
Public Folder Affinity   138
Where Do We Go from Here?   140
For Review   140

Chapter 8   Address Book Views   **143**

Global Address List   143
Address Book View   145
Creating Address Book Views   147
Using Address Book Views   150

Where Do We Go from Here?   152
For Review   152

Chapter 9   Clients   153

Microsoft Exchange Clients   153
Microsoft Outlook   155
Microsoft Schedule+   166
Microsoft Outlook Express   167
Microsoft Internet Mail and News   168
Outlook Web Access   168
Where Do We Go from Here?   170
For Review   170

Chapter 10   Connectors   173

Overview of Connectors   174
Addressing   174
Routing   178
Connections Container   182
Site Connector   182
Dynamic RAS Connector   184
X.400 Connector   186
MS Mail Connector and Dirsync   188
Connector for cc:Mail   195
Where Do We Go from Here?   195
For Review   195

Chapter 11   The Internet   199

Internet Protocols   199
Configuring Protocols   206
Internet Mail Service   211
Internet News Service   217
Firewalls and Security   220
Where Do We Go from Here?   221
For Review   221

Chapter 12   Monitoring   223

Server Monitors   223
Link Monitors   229
Message Queues   232
Performance Monitor   233

Where Do We Go from Here?   235
For Review   235

Chapter 13   Maintenance   **237**

Database and Log Files   237
Database Maintenance   243
Performing Backups   244
Performance Optimizer   246
Troubleshooting Tools   248
Where Do We Go from Here?   250
For Review   250

Chapter 14   Miscellaneous   **253**

Migration   253
Export/Import   258
Domain Mapping   263
Chat Service   264
Cluster Server   264
Where Do We Go from Here?   265
For Review   265

Index   267

Acknowledgments

I would like to acknowledge and thank the following individuals for their assistance in this project:

- My editor, Michael Sprague of McGraw-Hill. Michael, I always enjoy doing books with you, even though each time we communicate it's usually only for a New York minute!

- My agent, David L. Rogelberg of Studio B. David. Thanks, David, for opening doors for me that I never realized were possible.

- My Internet Service Provider, Escape Communications Corp. (www.escape.ca). Thanks for graciously providing Web hosting services for my personal Web site. Hope you find your free copy of this book useful!

- Dave Kinnaman, MCSE, by whose permission a portion of the material in Chapter 1 was used.

- My readers, who have made my two previous books a success. May this new book also help you reach your career goals.

- My wife and editorial assistant, Ingrid, whose research, suggestions, and corrections have been of invaluable help as always. We're really riding Mac's motorcycle now, eh?

Mitch Tulloch, MCT, MCSE, B.Sc., Dip.Ed. www.mtit.com

CHAPTER 1

Introduction to This Study Guide

Plan Your MCSE Process

So you want to become a Microsoft Certified Systems Engineer (an MCSE) do you? Then you've made a good choice in purchasing this book because it is designed specifically to prepare you for a vital MCSE examination. And this chapter is designed to prepare you for planning the whole process of becoming an MCSE and to assist you to outline the unique process to prepare you to pass all your MCSE examinations.

According to Microsoft, "Microsoft Certified Systems Engineers design, install, support, and troubleshoot information systems. MCSEs are network gurus, support technicians, and operating system experts." This is a central information technology role with major responsibilities in today's computer networking world.

To prepare for such a major role, it takes a solid plan. You must know all your options. Therefore, let's begin the planning with a discussion of the components of the objective: the core exams and elective exams that lead to the MCSE certificate. After identifying the core and elective exams, the remainder of this section is devoted to dispelling several myths about MCSE exams that could derail your plan if you believed them.

Core and Elective Exams

Two tracks toward becoming an MCSE actually exist at this writing. However, the vast majority of candidates concentrate on the more recent track. The older track is based on Windows NT 3.51, and the newer track is based on Windows NT 4.0. Because the exams for Windows NT 3.51 have been scheduled for retirement, nothing more will be said about NT 3.51.

MICROSOFT WINDOWS NT 4.0 TRACK

This track consists of mastering four core exams and two elective exams. All the many current elective exams are presented after the core exams.

Core Requirements (Four Exams)

You must pass four exams to complete the core requirements for MCSE certification. Three of these exams are required, while for the fourth exam you have a choice.

The following three exams are required:

- 70-067: Implementing and Supporting Microsoft Windows NT Server 4.0

- 70-068: Implementing and Supporting Microsoft Windows NT Server 4.0 in the Enterprise

- 70-058: Networking Essentials
  You also must choose one exam from the following:

- 70-064: Implementing and Supporting Microsoft Windows 95

- 70-098: Implementing and Supporting Microsoft Windows 98

- 70-073: Microsoft Windows NT Workstation 4.0

Elective Requirements (Two Exams)

There are a large number of elective exams to choose from. You can choose to become expert on any two of these software products:

- SNA Server
- Systems Management Server
- SQL Server
- TCP/IP on Microsoft Windows NT
- Exchange Server
- Internet Information Server

- Proxy Server
- Explorer 4.0 by Using the Internet Explorer Administration Kit.

CAUTION
Microsoft allows you to use, as electives, exams for one or two or three versions of several software products. Only one exam per product, regardless of version, can be counted toward the two-elective requirement. For example, if you pass both 70-013: Implementing and Supporting Microsoft SNA Server *version 3.0,* and 70-085: Implementing and Supporting Microsoft SNA Server *version4.0,* these two exams will only count for one elective. *The point is that passing exams on two versions of one product will not count as two electives—just one will count as an elective.*

One of these:

- 70-013: Implementing and Supporting Microsoft SNA Server 3.0
- 70-085: Implementing and Supporting Microsoft SNA Server 4.0

or one of these:

- 70-018: Implementing and Supporting Microsoft Systems Management Server 1.2
- 70-086: Implementing and Supporting Microsoft Systems Management Server 2.0

or one of these:

- 70-021: Microsoft SQL Server 4.2 Database Implementation (scheduled for retirement)
- 70-027: Implementing a Database Design on Microsoft SQL Server 6.5
- 70-029: Implementing a Database Design on Microsoft SQL Server 7.0

or one of these:

- 70-022: Microsoft SQL Server 4.2 Database Administration for Microsoft Windows NT (scheduled for retirement)

- 70-026: System Administration for Microsoft SQL Server 6.5
- 70-028: System Administration for Microsoft SQL Server 7.0

or one of these:

- 70-053: Internetworking Microsoft TCP/IP on Microsoft Windows NT (3.5-3.51)
- 70-059: Internetworking with Microsoft TCP/IP on Microsoft Windows NT 4.0

or one of these:

- 70-076: Implementing and Supporting Microsoft Exchange Server 5
- 70-081: Implementing and Supporting Microsoft Exchange Server 5.5

or one of these:

- 70-077: Implementing and Supporting Microsoft Internet Information Server 3.0 and Microsoft Index Server 1.1
- 70-087: Implementing and Supporting Microsoft Internet Information Server 4.0

or one of these:

- 70-078: Implementing and Supporting Microsoft Proxy Server 1.0
- 70-088: Implementing and Supporting Microsoft Proxy Server 2.0

or

- 70-079: Implementing and Supporting Microsoft Internet Explorer 4.0 by Using the Internet Explorer Administration Kit

With all these options available, MCSE candidates surely can find elective exams that fit their own career and workplace goals.

Required Software and Hardware

Many current MCSE holders earned their certificates at little or no out-of-pocket expense to themselves because their employers paid the costs for both training and exams. Many of them also did all or almost all their exam preparation on the clock, so their employers actually paid them to get an MCSE certificate. These fortunate MCSEs didn't even have to pay for software or equipment, because their employers also supplied appropriate software and hardware needed to practice all the skills necessary for their MCSE exams. If your employer offers this kind of comprehensive support, wonderful. However, if your employer expects you to pay your way to the MCSE entirely by yourself, here are some thoughts on what you'll need.

REQUIRED SOFTWARE

In most cases you'll need at least one copy of both the server and the client software, because most MCSE exams are about administering networks that contain the software in question. You'll need to know how the product works from both the client and administrator points of view, even if the exam is specifically about a client software, such as Windows NT 4.0 Workstation. As just mentioned, the MCSE exams are usually from the system support and administrator's point of view rather than from the client user's point of view.

Installing a Microsoft client software, of course, may require a preexisting operating system or a previous version of the client software, depending on the product involved. Similarly, several Microsoft server operating systems will require you to have *other* server operating systems already available on the network or installed and underlying on the server computer. This means that more than one server software program may be required for you to use and become familiar with all the tested features of the server software required for the exam.

The following hardware requirements are the bare minimum for systems used to practice and prepare for the core MCSE exams. Note that systems used to practice and prepare for elective exams (e.g., IIS 4.0) may have much higher hardware requirements.

MINIMUM REQUIRED HARDWARE

One or more Windows NT Workstation computers:

- 12 MB RAM
- VGA video
- Keyboard

- IDE, EIDE, SCSI, or ESDI hard disk
- 486/25 processor or faster
- 124 MB free hard drive space [recommended minimum: over 300 MB, including a copy of the entire I386 installation directory (223 MB) plus Windows 95 or DOS 6.22]. For hard disk controllers using translation mode to address the drive, increase these minimum sizes by 80 MB.
- CD-ROM drive, or a floppy disk drive and an active network connection

One or more Windows NT Server computers:

- 16 MB RAM (32 MB or more recommended)
- VGA video
- Keyboard
- IDE, EIDE, SCSI, or ESDI hard disk
- 486/25 processor (486DX2/50 or better preferred)
- 124 MB free hard drive space [recommended minimum: over 300 MB, including a copy of the entire I386 installation directory (223 MB) plus Windows 95 or DOS 6.22]. For hard disk controllers using translation mode to address the drive, increase these minimum sizes by 80 MB.
- CD-ROM drive (Windows NT compatible recommended), or a floppy disk drive and an active network connection
- Recommended: 28.8 v.34 (or faster) external modem, for remote debugging and troubleshooting

Costs to Obtain an MCSE

As mentioned earlier, the costs of an MCSE certificate are invisible to many current certificate holders because the costs are entirely supported by their employers. Because these advanced skills are of great value to the workplace, it is appropriate that employers provide this support, in exchange for more efficient and more productive work skills.

Some supportive employers do require a contract, to assure themselves that the newly trained MCSE will not change jobs to another employer shortly after obtaining the MCSE certificate— presumably before the current employer has had time to recoup the costs of the MCSE for their former employee. These contracts typically require the employee to repay MCSE costs on a prorated basis depending on how long the MCSE candidate remained with the former employer. Often the new employer picks up the costs of buying out the former employer's training contract as a part of the new and more advantageous employment agreement.

Note that MCSE holders are considered more employable and therefore more mobile in their employment. The cost efficiency of information technology workplaces has been hard hit by a mercenary, contract-worker mentality that drains the spirit from workers. In contrast, employers who provide an environment of mutual trust and employment security, by fostering loyalty and good will in all employees, will obtain the best return on their investment in employee MCSE training.

MCSE Expense Budget	Costs
Examinations	$600 (retests at $100 each)
Training, seminars, workshops	
Study time	
Books and materials	
Practice examination software	
Network hardware, network analysis equipment	
Server and client hardware	
Server and client software	

MCSE Myth No. 1—Everyone Must Take Six Exams to Earn the MCSE

Reality—Some People Are Exempt from One Exam

Some networking professionals are exempt from taking the Networking Essentials exam because they already passed a similarly rigorous exam through Novell, Banyan, Sun, or Microsoft. These professionals are already skilled and possess certificates to prove it. Microsoft grants them MCSE certificates after they pass only five additional Microsoft exams. Specifically, Microsoft automatically grants credit for the Networking Essentials exam once you've passed a Microsoft Certified Professional (MCP) exam and provide evidence that you hold one of these exact certificates:

Novell

CNE—Certified Novell Engineer

CNI—Certified Novell Instructor

ECNE—Enterprise Certified Novell Engineer

MCNE—Master Certified Novell Engineer

Banyan

CBE—Certified Banyan CBE

CBS—Certified Banyan Specialist

Sun

CNA—Sun Certified Network Administrators for Solaris 2.5

CNA—Sun Certified Network Administrators for Solaris 2.6

Therefore, if you already hold one of the preceding certificates, just pass one MCP exam and provide proof of your previous networking certificate, and you'll receive credit for two exams for the price of one.

WHAT'S AN MCP EXAM?

An MCP exam is a Microsoft exam first of all. Passing an MCP exam makes you a Microsoft Certified Professional and automatically enrolls you in the Microsoft MCP program. However, not all Microsoft exams are MCP exams. Networking Essentials, for instance, is not an MCP exam. The sidebar has more information about the MCP designation.

MICROSOFT CERTIFIED PROFESSIONALS (MCPs)

Microsoft Certified Professional (MCP) is Microsoft's entry-level certification. An MCP is an individual who has demonstrated expertise in any Microsoft product by passing a Microsoft exam in that product. You become an MCP as soon as you pass your first Microsoft exam. Formerly, that exam had to be an operating system exam, but as of October 1, 1998, passing any Microsoft exam except Exam 70-058: Networking Essentials, qualifies you to immediately become an MCP.

MCP Benefits

- *Industry recognition* that you possess knowledge and proficiency with Microsoft products and technologies
- *Access to technical and product information* through a secured MCP Web site
- *MCP logos* that you can use on your business card, letterhead, or Web site to identify your MCP status to colleagues and clients
- *Invitations* to Microsoft events, conferences, and training sessions
- *An MCP certificate* you can hang on your wall
- *Free subscription to Microsoft Certified Professional Magazine,* a magazine for the professional development of MCPs (Postage charges apply outside the United States.)

For more information, visit the Microsoft Certified Professional Web site—Certification Home Page

http://www.microsoft.com/mcp

By taking an MCP exam early in the MCSE process, you can gain access to the MCP benefits just mentioned, which are valuable to obtaining an MCSE as well.

Two Retired Microsoft Exams May Substitute for Networking Essentials

In addition to the networking certificates listed earlier from Novell, Banyan, and Sun that can substitute for passing the Networking Essentials exam, there are two more ways to achieve an MCSE with only five (additional) exams. If you happen to have taken and passed one of the following two retired Microsoft exams, you can use that previous exam to have the Networking Essentials exam MCSE requirement waived.

- Exam 70-046: Networking with Microsoft Windows for Workgroups 3.11 (retired)
- Exam 70-047: Networking with Microsoft Windows 3.1 (retired)

Retired Microsoft exams are explained in detail later in this chapter.

MCSE Myth No. 2—Only One Year to Finish
Reality—Take as Long as You Like to Finish Your MCSE

Take as much time as you need to be prepared for each test. There is no stated time limit for completion of the MCSE certificate. Begin, and take examinations when you are ready. Although there is a popular misconception that you have only 1 year (or 2 years, or *whatever*) to complete your MCSE certificate, there is in fact no time limit. The only limits are your own motivation and the time available in your life. As an adult, you can decide for yourself how much more of your life you want to spend working as something other than an MCSE.

Therefore, you should plan to progress at your own deliberate or expeditious speed depending on your needs, your personal learning style, and the amount of time, money, and concentration you can devote to this project. Everyone starts their MCSE studies with different personal backgrounds, different circumstances, and different knowledge. Each reader has different expectations for this book. Some readers will want a guide

- To confirm that they already know enough to be certified.

- To accompany a class or even a crash course.

- To study on their own, reading and applying the concepts as they go.

Not having an MCSE time limit is also consistent with good educational design, because adults learn best at their own rates and in their own ways. It also keeps Microsoft away from the "bad guy" enforcer role. This way Microsoft never has to say, "Sorry, all your work was for nothing, you're too late—you must start over."

CAUTION

There is a possible down side to extending your MCSE studies. The longer you take, the more likely it is that one of the exams you've already passed will be retired *before* you finish your MCSE studies. If an exam you've passed is retired while you are still pursuing your MCSE, you'll need to replace the retired exam with a current exam, causing you more work to accomplish the same original goal.

Another reason to progress toward your MCSE with all due dispatch is in recognition of your own personal learning style. Many adults learn best if they concentrate heavily on learning, passing exams as a kind of punctuation in their study cycle. Also, each exam has areas of overlap with other exams. What you learn for one exam will help with other exams as well. Taking Exam B soon after taking Exam A, while the learning for Exam A is still fresh in your memory, can be ideal for some adult learners. Adjust your exam strategy to accommodate your own learning style.

MCSE Myth No. 3—Two-Week Wait for a Retest

Reality—First Retest Anytime, Second Retest after 2 Weeks

Although several changes have been instituted to improve security around the MCSE exams, until now it is still okay to retake a failed exam as soon as you want. Therefore, if it happens that

- you fell asleep during the exam,

- you just had a bad day and only missed passing by one question,

- you were coming down with the flu the day of the exam, or

- you otherwise failed an exam in a fluke event that did not represent your true level of mastery of the material,

then you can reschedule the same exam and retest as soon as you please—at full price, of course. If you fail twice, however, you will be required to wait at least 2 weeks before trying a third time.

TEST TIP

Many MCSE candidates and MCSE certificate holders are convinced that certain questions appear on more than one exam. It seems to others that one or two questions are pulled from their "mother" exam and placed at random on other exams without a discernible pattern. They claim that questions they expected on the TCP/IP exam turned up on the Windows NT Server or the Enterprise exam, for instance. Building a strong personal foundation of knowledge and experience is the only defense against this sort of random substitution, if it occurs.

It is clear that the exams are at least quasi-hierarchical, in that almost all Windows NT Workstation exam questions are legitimate fodder for the Windows NT Server exam and all Windows NT Server exam questions are fair game for the Windows NT Server in the Enterprise exam, for instance. Likewise, all Networking Essentials questions are also fair game on the TCP/IP exam. This is another reason to take the exams in a deliberate, thoughtful order that makes sense with your own experience and knowledge.

MCSE Myth No. 4—You Must Pass Exam A *before* Exam B

Reality—There Is No Required Exam Sequence

WHICH EXAM SHOULD YOU TAKE FIRST?

Please understand that there is no required sequence at all. You can literally take the MCSE exams in any order you please and achieve your certificate with no prejudice based on the procession of your exams. However, there are good reasons why you might want to consider a purposeful sequence rather than a random sequence of tests.

Here is a sample way to plan your studies. It is based on three assumptions, which may or may not be true for you. First, the assumptions are

1. That you aren't already certifiable in one or more exam areas.

2. That you don't have more extensive experience and knowledge in some exam areas than the others.

3. That you've decided to take these six exams, for example, to satisfy the requirements for the MCSE:

   - Example core requirements:
     - 70-058: Networking Essentials
     - 70-067: Implementing and Supporting Microsoft Windows NT Server 4.0
     - 70-068: Implementing and Supporting Microsoft Windows NT Server 4.0 in the Enterprise
     - 70-073: Implementing and Supporting Microsoft Windows NT Workstation 4.0

   - Example elective requirements:
     - 70-059: Internetworking with Microsoft TCP/IP on Windows NT 4.0
     - 70-081: Implementing and Supporting Microsoft Exchange Server 5.5

If these exams and givens fit your case, you might want to proceed in one of the exam sequences suggested below. First, check out the sidebar for basic suggestions for sequencing all MCSE exams:

SUGGESTIONS FOR MCSE EXAM SEQUENCING

- Take the exam(s) you are *already* better prepared for first, if possible, to get things rolling and to begin your benefits as an MCP. Current Microsoft MCP benefits are summarized in another sidebar.
- Take the more fundamental exam first, if one exam is a building block for another exam. This allows you to begin laying the conceptual and learning foundation for more complex ideas.
- Take exams that have fair to high overlaps in Table 1-1 one after the other, if possible.
- Take exams that will be easiest for you either at the beginning or at the end of the sequence or as a deliberate break between tougher exams that are more challenging to you.

Table 1-1 Some Exams Overlap More than Others*

Perceived Exam Overlaps	Net- working Essentials	Windows NT Work- station	Windows NT Server	NT Server in the Enter- prise	TCP/IP
NT Work- station	Low				
NT Server	Low	High			
NT Server/ Enterprise	Fair	Low	High		
TCP/IP	High	Low	Low	Low	
IIS 4.0	Low	Low	Fair	Fair	High
Windows 98	Low	Low	Low	Low	Fair
Exchange Server 5.5	Low	Low	Fair	Fair	Low

*The Windows NT Server and the Windows NT Server in the Enterprise Exams have a high degree of overlap.

ENTERPRISE, SERVER, WORKSTATION

Table 1-1 estimates the overlap of content and knowledge areas between several popular exams. Of these, the three most closely related exams are

- Windows NT Workstation
- Windows NT Server
- Windows NT Server in the Enterprise

It makes sense to take these three exams in that order (Workstation, Server, and Enterprise), unless you already have extensive or special expertise in Windows NT Server or Windows NT Server in the Enterprise.

Of the exams listed in Table 1-1, these four are generally considered to be the toughest:

- Windows NT Server in the Enterprise
- TCP/IP on Microsoft Windows NT (any version)
- Windows 95 or 98
- Exchange Server 5.5

As usual, the exam that will be the toughest for you is the exam for which you are unprepared.

TCP/IP, NETWORKING ESSENTIALS, AND IIS

The next strongest relationship among the exams is the high degree of overlap between TCP/IP and both the Networking Essentials exams and the IIS exam. Because Networking Essentials is considered the foundation of standards and definitions needed for networking concepts used in other exams, Networking Essentials is often taken early in the exam sequence.

As already mentioned, TCP/IP is judged to be one of the more difficult exams, even after the exam was redesigned to moderate the impact of subnetting.

IIS 3.0 commonly was considered one of the more straightforward MCSE exams, largely because MCSE candidates are familiar with how to prepare for Microsoft exams by the time they attempt this exam. However, the exam on the newer version IIS 4.0 is somewhat more difficult because of the wider range of material covered and the new user interface (the Microsoft Management Console). Nevertheless, if you are contemplating taking either of these exams, it would be best for you to take the IIS 4.0 exam, since certification in this exam is likely to remain current for a longer period of time, and the IIS 3.0 exam likely will be retired when NT 5.0 comes out.

Therefore, combining all these information sources, here are some acceptable proposed exam sequences:

Exam Sequence A

1. Networking Essentials
2. Workstation
3. Server
4. Enterprise
5. TCP/IP
6. IIS

Exam Sequence B

1. Networking Essentials
2. TCP/IP
3. Workstation
4. Server
5. IIS
6. Enterprise

Exam Sequence C

1. Workstation
2. Networking Essentials
3. Server
4. Enterprise
5. TCP/IP
6. IIS

If you selected other exams for your MCSE rather than the six used in these examples, use these same principles to find your own ideal exam sequence.

TEST TIP

It is not uncommon for networking professionals, with years of actual experience, to fail the Networking Essentials exam. Likewise, it is often heard that the TCP/IP exam is considered tough by seasoned Internet experts. Why is this so?

The most satisfying explanation is that these professionals already *know too much* about real-world networking, and they "read into" the exams real-world facts that are not stated in the questions. Many Microsoft exam questions are stated ambiguously, and the resulting vagueness seems to force these professionals to make assumptions. They assume that if the question says X, and they know that X is almost always because of Y, that Z must be true—only to find that Z is not even an available answer!

Network professionals advise that for their colleagues taking the Networking Essentials or TCP/IP exams from Microsoft, nothing from the real world should be assumed. Read the questions at face value only, to avoid reading anything real into the question. Often the questions that are the most troubling to these experts are simply testing their factual knowledge rather than testing their troubleshooting expertise and network design experience.

Therefore, networking professionals with extensive prior experience often hold these two exams (Networking Essentials and TCP/IP) to the end of their exam sequence, hoping to get into the flow of the Microsoft testing manner of thinking before encountering these too familiar topics.

BETA EXAMS ARE HALF PRICE!

When a new exam is under construction, Microsoft *tests* the exam questions on folks like you and me. For $50, rather than the regular, full price of $100, you or I can take, and possibly pass, an exam while it is still in its "beta" stage.

You should expect beta exams to have between 150 and 200 questions, because they contain all the questions being considered for all versions of that exam. On a beta exam, you'll have *only* 3 hours to answer all the questions. This means that on a beta exam you must work at least at the same rapid pace you would use on a regular exam, if not faster.

Although beta exams can save you some money, they also can be frustrating, because it takes 6 to 8 weeks to get your scores back from Microsoft. Waiting that long can be quite a trauma when you're used to having immediate results as you leave the testing room!

Important—Please Note: Beta exams are designated with a 71 at the beginning of the exam code number rather than the regular exam codes, which begin with a 70.

To find out if any beta exams are available, check this URL:

MCP Exam Information:

http://www.microsoft.com/mcp/examinfo/exams.htm

Another point should be made about the Web page just cited. The dynamic links on the page jump to the official Microsoft Preparation Guides for each upcoming examination. Notice that the Preparation Guides become available *even before* the beta exams. This means you can actually be studying for an exam at the same time that they're preparing the exam to test your skills.

However, to study before the beta exam exists sometimes requires you to have access to the beta software product on which the exam is based. One of the many benefits of obtaining an MCSE certificate is a 1-year subscription to the Microsoft Beta Evaluation program—free monthly CDs containing Microsoft beta software.

As of December 1998, the following exam is available in beta form:

- 70-100: Analyzing Requirements and Defining Solution Architectures

The following exams will be available shortly in beta form:

- 70-019: Designing and Implementing Data Warehouses with Microsoft SQL Server 7.0 (to appear in beta in second quarter 1999)
- 70-028: System Administration for Microsoft SQL Server 7.0 (to appear in beta in February 1999)
- 70-029: Designing and Implementing Databases with Microsoft SQL Server 7.0 (to appear in beta in February 1999)
- 70-086: Implementing and Supporting Microsoft Systems Management Server 2.0 (to appear in beta in March 1999)

Old Exams Are Eventually Retired

Yes, Microsoft retires old exams. However, they take several specific measures to mollify the effect of obsolete exams on certified professionals—including giving 6 months advanced warning in writing and substantially cutting the cost of replacement exams for at least 6 months *after* the former exam is retired. Read on for the details.

When an operating system (OS) is no longer commonly in use, supporting the old operating system becomes increasingly expensive. If new and better operating systems are available at reasonable prices and the migration path for the majority of users is not too burdensome, it stands to reason that the manufacturer would want to withdraw the old OS from support. Similarly, Microsoft examinations are withdrawn and retired when their use has waned, especially when the OS they are based on is becoming obsolete.

In explaining Microsoft's policy on retirement of exams, it's useful to know that the company highly values the relevance of the *skills measured by the exams*. If your skills are still good in the marketplace, there will be less reason to retire the exam that certified those skills. Microsoft explains that their exam retirement decisions are based on several factors, including

- Total number of copies of the product ever sold (the customer base)
- Total number of exams ever taken (the MCP base)
- Ongoing sales of corresponding Microsoft products
- Ongoing sales of corresponding Microsoft courseware

By considering this broad framework, Microsoft can retire only exams which have fallen from use and have truly become obsolete.

Microsoft announces which exams are being withdrawn and retired at this URL:

Microsoft Certified Professional Web site—Retired MCP Exams Information: http://www.microsoft.com/mcp/examinfo/retired.htm

If your MCSE certificate is based on an exam that is being or has been retired, you'll probably need to find a replacement exam to prepare for and pass to position your certificate for renewal.

WHAT HAPPENS WHEN ONE OF MY EXAMS IS RETIRED?

Although there are no guarantees that these policies will always be the same, here are the current Microsoft policies on exam retirements:

- First, you'll be mailed a notification in writing at least 6 months *before* your certification is affected.

- You'll be given a date deadline by which to pass specific replacement exam(s).

- You may take all replacement exams at a 50 percent discount until at least 6 months after the exam retirement date.

For any questions or comments about Microsoft exam retirements, or if you ever want to check your certification status or ask about the MCSE program in general, just send e-mail to mcp@msprograms.com or call one of the regional education centers below:

Microsoft Regional Education Centers

North America	800-636-7544
Asia and Pacific	61-2-9870-2250
Europe	353-1-7038774
Latin America	801-579-2829

In addition, there are many more toll-free numbers for Microsoft International Training & Certification Customer Service Centers in several dozen countries worldwide at this URL:

Microsoft Training & Certification Programs—International Training and Certification Customer Service Centers http://www.microsoft.com/train_cert/resc.htm

One more thought on retiring exams: Because an MCSE certificate is good for life, or until exams are retired, the *only way* to be sure that MCSE professionals are keeping up with the real-world information technology market is for Microsoft to retire exams. For the MCSE to continue to signify the highest level of professional skills, old exams must be retired and replaced with more current exams based on skills currently in demand.

TEST TIP

One of the earliest warnings that an exam you've taken may become obsolete is that the development of a new exam is announced for the next version of the software or a beta exam is announced for a new version of the exam. Once beta software or a beta exam has appeared, watch for further signs more closely.

Usually there is advanced warning that an exam is being withdrawn many months before the event. If you subscribe to the following monthly mailing lists and read the Web pages mentioned, you'll have the longest forewarning to choose how you'll prepare for any changes.

- *MCP News Flash* (monthly)—Includes exam announcements and special promotions
- *Training and Certification News* (monthly)—About training and certification at Microsoft

To subscribe to either newsletter, visit this Web page, register with Microsoft, and then subscribe:

Personal Information Center
    http://207.46.130.169/regwiz/forms/PICWhyRegister.htm

Don't be caught off guard. Stay in touch with the status of the MCSE exams you've invested in mastering!

FREE SAMPLE EXAM SOFTWARE CD-ROM

Microsoft will ship [by United Parcel Service (UPS) so an ordinary U.S. Postal Service post office box address won't work] a CD containing a dated snapshot of the Microsoft Certified Professional (MCP) Web site and sample examination software called Personal Exam Prep (PEP) exams.

By calling Microsoft in the United States or Canada at 800-636-7544, you can request the most recent CD of the MCP Web site. *Ask for the "Roadmap CD."* The person to whom you are speaking may protest greatly—don't worry. He or she will say that the *"Roadmap to Certification CD"* is no longer available and that you would be much better off to check the Microsoft Web site for more up-to-date information. However, he or she also will still (as of this writing) ship a CD if you insist, and if you provide an address *other than a post office box.*

Of course, if you're in a hurry, you can always download the free sample exam software directly from the Microsoft Web site at

Personal Exam Prep (PEP) Tests
    http://www.microsoft.com/mcp/examinfo/practice.htm
    (mspep.exe) (561K)

The free PEP exam download currently covers these Microsoft tests:

- 70-018: Implementing and Supporting Microsoft® Systems Management Server 1.2
- 70-026: System Administration for Microsoft SQL Server™ 6.5
- 70-027: Implementing a Database Design on Microsoft SQL Server 6.5
- 70-059: Internetworking with Microsoft TCP/IP on Microsoft Windows NT 4.0
- 70-058: Networking Essentials
- 70-059: Internetworking with Microsoft TCP/IP on Microsoft Windows NT 4.0
- 70-063: Implementing and Supporting Microsoft Windows 95
- 70-064: Implementing and Supporting Microsoft Windows 95
- 70-067: Implementing and Supporting Microsoft Windows NT Server 4.0
- 70-068: Implementing and Supporting Microsoft Windows NT Server 4.0 in the Enterprise
- 70-073: Implementing and Supporting Microsoft Windows NT Workstation 4.0
- 70-075: Implementing and Supporting Microsoft Exchange Server 4.0
- 70-076: Implementing and Supporting Microsoft Exchange Server 5.0
- 70-077: Implementing and Supporting Microsoft Internet Information Server 3.0 and Microsoft Index Server 1.1
- 70-085: Implementing and Supporting Microsoft SNA Server 4.0
- 70-087: Implementing and Supporting Microsoft Internet Information Server 4.0
- 70-160: Microsoft Windows Architecture I
- 70-161: Microsoft Windows Architecture II
- 70-165: Developing Applications with Microsoft Visual Basic 5.0 Free Personal Exam Prep (PEP) Test Software

The PEP sample exam software has many values. First, you should take the appropriate PEP exam as the *beginning* of your studies for each new exam. This mere act commits you to the course of study for that exam and offers you a valid taste of the depth and breadth of the real exam. Seeing what kind of material is on the exams also allows you to recognize the actual level of detail expected on the exams so that you can avoid studying too much or studying too little to pass the exam.

Later, by taking the PEP examination again from time to time, you can generally gauge your progress through the material. The PEP exam also gives you practice at taking an exam on a computer. Perhaps best of all, it allows you to print the questions and answers for items you may have missed so that you can concentrate on areas where your understanding is weakest.

Although the PEP tests are written by Self Test Software, they are distributed free by Microsoft to assist MCP candidates in preparing for the real exams. Take advantage of this generous offer! Several other sources of practice exam software, including several more free samples, are provided later in this chapter.

Prepare for Each Exam

Free TechNet CD

The value of this offer cannot be overestimated. The free TechNet Trial CD includes the entire Microsoft knowledge base, plus many evaluation and deployment guides, white papers, and all the text from the Microsoft resource kits. This information is straight from the horse's mouth and therefore is indispensable to your successful studies for the MCSE certificate. And the price can't be beat. Do not delay, get this free TechNet CD today!

Of course, Microsoft is hoping you'll actually subscribe to TechNet. Once you have earned the MCSE certificate, you probably will be sure to convince your employer to subscribe, if you don't subscribe yourself. TechNet can help you solve obscure problems more quickly, it can help you keep up to date with fast-paced technology developments inside and outside Microsoft, and it can help you keep your bosses and your users happy.

Microsoft TechNet ITHome—Get a Free TechNet Trial Subscription
  http://204.118.129.122/giftsub/Clt1Form.asp

On the same Web page you also can register for ITHome and other free newsletters.

Remember, Microsoft exams generally don't require you to recall obscure information. Common networking situations and ordinary administrative tasks are the real focus. Exam topics include common circumstances, ordinary issues, and popular network problems that networking and operating system experts are confronted with every day.

Use Practice Exams

Taking a practice exam early helps you focus your study on the topics and level of detail appropriate for the exam. As mentioned earlier, taking another practice exam later can help you gauge how well your studies are progressing. Many professionals wait until their practice exams scores are well above the required passing score for that exam, and then they take the real exam.

There are many sources of practice exams, and most of the vendors offer free samples of some kind. Microsoft supplies free samples exam from Self Test Software, and the MCSE mailing lists on the Internet often recommend products from Transcender. Both of these and several other practice exam sources are listed in the sidebar.

PRACTICE EXAMS AVAILABLE—FREE SAMPLES!

BeachFrontQuizzer
Email: info@bfq.com
http://www.bfq.com/
Phone: 888-992-3131

A free practice exam (for Windows NT 4.0 Workstation) is available for download.

LearnKey
http://www.learnkey.com/
Phone: 800-865-0165
Fax: 435-674-9734
1845 W. Sunset Blvd.
St. George, UT 84770-6508

MasterExam simulation software—$800 for six exam simulations, or $150 each.

NetG
info@netg.com
support@netg.com
http://www.netg.com/
800-265-1900 (in United States only)
630-369-3000
Fax: 630-983-4518

NETg International
info@uk.netg.com
1 Hogarth Business Park
Burlington Lane
Chiswick, London
England W4 2TJ
Phone: 0181-994-4404
Fax: 0181-994-5611

Supporting Microsoft Windows NT 4.0 Core Technologies, Part 1 (course 71410, unit 1, 7.7 MB), and Microsoft FrontPage Fundamentals (course 71101, unit 2, 8.1 MB) are available as free sample downloads.

Prep Technologies, Inc.
Sales@mcpprep.com
Support@mcpprep.com
http://www.mcpprep.com/
1-888-627-7737 (1-888-MCP-PREP)
1-708-478-8684 (outside US)

CICPreP (Computer Industry Certification Preparation from ITS, Inc)

A free 135-question practice exam is available for download (5+ MB).

Self Test Software
feedback@stsware.com
http://www.stsware.com/

Americas
Toll-Free: 1-800-244-7330 (Canada and USA)
Elsewhere: 1-770-641-1489
Fax 1-770-641-9719

Self Test Software Inc.
4651 Woodstock Road
Suite 203, M/S 384
Roswell, GA 30075-1686

Australia/Asia
Email address stsau@vue.com
Phone: 61-2-9320-5497
Fax: 61-2-9323-5590
Sydney, Australia

Europe/Africa
The Netherlands
Phone: 31-348-484646
Fax: 31-348-484699

$79 for the first practice exam, $69 for additional practice exams ordered at the same time.

Twelve free practice exams are available for download. These are the same free practice exams that Microsoft distributes by download or CD.

Transcender
Product questions: sales@transcender.com
Technical support questions: support@transcender.com
Demo download problems: troubleshooting@transcender.com
http://www.transcender.com/
Phone 615-726-8779
Fax 615-726-8884
621 Mainstream Drive Suite 270
Nashville, TN 37228-1229

Fifteen free practice exams are available for download.

VFX Technologies, Inc
sales@vfxtech.com
support@vfxtech.com
http://www.vfxtech.com/
Phone 610-265.9222
Fax 610-265.6007
POB 80222
Valley Forge, PA 19484-0222 USA

Twenty-two free practice MCP Endeavor exam preparation modules are available for download.

Organize before the Day of the Exam

Make sure you have plenty of time to study before each exam. You know yourself. Give yourself enough time to both study *and* get plenty of sleep for at least 2 days before the exam. Make sure coworkers, family, and friends are aware of the importance of this effort so that they will give you the time and space to devote to your studies.

Once you have the materials and equipment you need and study times and locations properly selected—force yourself to study and practice. Reward yourself when you finish a segment or unit of studying. Pace yourself so that you complete your study plan on time.

Survey Testing Centers

Call each testing center in your area to find out what times they offer Microsoft exams. Jot down the center's name, address, and phone number, along with the testing hours and days of the week. Once you've checked the testing hours at all the centers in your local area, you're in a better position to schedule an exam at Center B if Center A is already booked for the time you wanted to take your next exam.

The Sylvan technician taking your registration may not easily find all other testing centers near you, so be prepared to suggest alternative testing center names for the technician to locate, in the event that your first choice is not available.

Plan to take your MCSE exams at a time of your own choice, after you know when exams are available in your area. This puts you in control and allows you to take into account your own life situation and your own style. If you are sharpest in the early morning, take the exams in the morning. If you can't get calm enough for an exam until late afternoon, schedule your exams for whatever time of day or phase of the moon that best suits you. If you really need to have a "special" time slot, schedule your exam well in advance.

Same-Day and Weekend Testing

You may be able to schedule an exam on the same day that you call to register—if you're lucky. This special service requires the test vendor, Sylvan or VUE, to download the exam to the testing site especially for you, and it requires the testing site to have an open slot at a time acceptable to you. Sometimes this works out, and sometimes it doesn't. Most testing centers are interested in filling all available exam time slots, so if you get a wild hair to take an exam *today*, why not give it a try? VUE testing centers can schedule exams for you, so they are especially well positioned for same-day testing.

Shop Around for the Best Testing Center Available

Shop around your area for the best testing center. Some testing centers are distractingly busy and noisy at all times. Some official testing centers have slow 25-MHz computers, small 12-in monitors, cramped seating conditions, or distracting activity outside the windows of the testing rooms. Some centers occasionally even have crabby, uninformed staff. Some centers actually limit testing to certain hours or certain days of the week rather than allowing testing during all open hours.

Because these MCSE exams are important to your career—you deserve to use the best testing environment available. The best center costs the same $100 that a less pleasant center does. Shop around and find out exactly what is available in your area.

If you are treated improperly, or if appropriate services or accommodations were not available when they should have been, let Sylvan or VUE, and Microsoft, know by e-mail and telephone.

Check for Aviation Testing Centers

Some of the best testing centers are actually at airports! Aviation training centers, located at all major airports to accommodate pilots, frequently are well-equipped and pleasant environments. Aviation training centers participate in Microsoft testing in order to better use their investment in computer testing rooms and to broaden their customer base.

The best thing about aviation training centers is that they are regularly open all day on weekends, both Saturday and Sunday. The staff at some aviation training centers actually like to work on weekends! One verified example, for instance, of an aviation training center and excellent Microsoft testing center available all day every weekend is Wright Flyers in San Antonio, Texas (telephone: 210-820-3800 or e-mail: Wflyers@Flash.Net).

Official Exam Registration and Scheduling

VUE exam scheduling and rescheduling services are available on weekends and evenings; in fact, VUE is open on the World Wide

Web 24 hours a day, 365 days a year. Sylvan's telephone hours are Monday through Friday 7:00 A.M. through 7:00 P.M. Central Time, and the new Saturday telephone hours are 7:00 A.M. through 3:00 P.M.

As mentioned earlier, many testing centers are open weekends on both Saturday and Sunday. If something goes horribly wrong at a Sylvan testing center after 3:00 P.M. on Saturday or anytime on Sunday—you'll have to wait to talk to Sylvan until Monday morning. As has happened, if a testing center simply fails to open its doors for your scheduled exam while Sylvan is closed for the weekend, you can do nothing until Monday morning.

Install the Software and Try Each Option

Make sure you know the layout of the various options in the software's graphic user interface (GUI) and which popular configuration options are set on each menu. Become "GUI familiar" with each software product required in your next exam by opening and studying each and every option on each and every menu. Also, for whatever they're worth, read the Help files, especially any context-sensitive Help!

Commonly tested everyday network features, such as controlling access to sensitive resources, printing over the network, client and server software installation, configuration, troubleshooting, load balancing, fault tolerance, and combinations of these topics (e.g., security-sensitive printing over the network), are especially important. Remember, the exams are from the network administrator's point of view. Imagine what issues network designers, technical support specialists, and network administrators are faced with every day—these are the issues that will be hit hardest on the exams.

MCSE candidates are expected to be proficient at planning, renovating, and operating Microsoft networks that are well integrated with Novell networks, with IBM LANs and IBM mainframes, with network printers (with their own network interface cards), and with other common network services. Microsoft expects you to be able to keep older products, especially older Microsoft products, running as long as possible and to know when they finally must be upgraded and how to accomplish the upgrade or migration with the least pain and expense.

Pass One Exam at a Time

Microsoft exams are experience-based and require real know-how, not just book learning. Don't be fooled by anyone—you must have real experience with the hardware and software involved to excel on the exams or as an MCSE certificate holder in the workplace.

Passing a Microsoft exam is mostly a statement that you have the experience and knowledge that are required. And there is also an element in passing of knowing how to deal with the exam situation, one question at a time. This section describes the various kinds of questions you'll encounter on the MCSE exams and gives you pointers and tips about successful strategies for dealing with each kind of question.

This section then walks you through the process of scheduling an exam, arriving at the test center, and taking the exam. There is also a brief resource list of additional sources of information related to topics in this chapter.

Choose the Best Answer

Questions of this type are the most popular because they are seemingly simple questions. "Choose the best answer" means *one* answer, but the fact that there is only one answer doesn't make the question easy—unless you know the material.

First, try to eliminate at least two obviously wrong answers. This narrows the field so that you can choose among the remaining options more easily.

TEST TIP

Briefly look at the exhibit when you *begin* to read the question. Note important features in the exhibit, and then finish a careful reading of the whole question. Then return to the exhibit after you've read the entire question to check on any relevant details revealed in the question.

Some exhibits have nothing to do with answering the question correctly, so don't waste your time on the exhibit if it has no useful information for finding the solution.

Choose All That Apply

The most obviously tough questions are those with an uncertain number of multiple choices: "Choose all that apply." Here, you should use the same procedure to eliminate wrong answers first. Select only the items which you have confidence in—don't be tempted to take a wild guess. Remember, the Microsoft exams do not allow partial credit for partial answers, so any wrong answer is deadly, even if you got the rest of it right!

Really Read the Scenario Questions!

There is no better advice for these killer questions. Read the scenario questions carefully and completely. These seemingly complex questions are composed of several parts, generally in this pattern:

1. First, there are always a few short paragraphs describing the situation, hardware, software, and organization involved, possibly including one or two exhibits that must be opened, studied, and then minimized or closed again.

2. The required results

3. Two or three optional desired results

4. The proposed solution

5. Four multiple-choice answers from which you must choose

   Pay close attention to the number of optional results specified in answer B

   Most scenario questions have an opening screen that warns that you should "Pay close attention to the number of optional results specified in answer B." This instruction is to accommodate the fact that there are sometimes two and sometimes three optional results and to accommodate occasional proposed solutions that only satisfy the required result and some (but not all) of the optional results.

   Often two scenario questions in a row will differ only in their proposed solution. They'll have the same test, the same exhibit, the same results, but different solutions will be proposed. Sometimes some other slight difference might be introduced in the second scenario. Compare these similar questions, noting the differences to see what's missing or what's new in the second question. If the second question satisfies all the required and desired results, this tends to imply that the *previous* scenario did not satisfy all optional results, at least.

Also, it is common to encounter another scenario question later in the same exam that clarifies the situation in the previous scenario. Some people jot down the question numbers and topics of each scenario to enable them to return and reconsider a question after reading other, related questions and perhaps having a flash of memory that might help.

TEST TIP

The scuttlebutt is that if you just don't have a clue on a complex scenario question, or if you're out of time, you should select answer A (meets all results) or D (meets none), because these are the most frequently correct answers. The recommended method, of course, is to know the material better so that you never need to resort to this kind of superstitious advantage.

For most people, your first priority should be to note the required results. If the proposed solution does not satisfy the required result, you're done with the question and you can move on. Thus there is no need to focus on the optional desired results unless the required result is satisfied.

There can be up to three optional desired results, and each one must be evaluated independently. Usually, if an optional result is satisfied, there are specific words in the question that deal with the optional result. Use the practice exams to sharpen your skills at quickly identifying which optional results are satisfied by which words in the question.

Another strategy that works for some people is to focus first on the question and results (both required and optional), writing down all related facts based on the question's wording. This strategy then evaluates the proposed solution, based on the previous question analysis. Because some people find the scenario questions to be ambiguously written and vague, this strategy also can lead to time wasted on unimportant or unnecessary analysis, especially if the proposed solution does not meet the required results.

Some people work at exams differently. Aside from intelligence, there are also very different learning and understanding styles among adults. Some people, for instance, find that they deal better with the scenario questions by working backwards from the required results and later, if necessary, from the optional results. They break the question into its elements, find their own solutions, and then finally compare notes with the solution proposed by the exam.

For example, they might start from the required results, building the case that would be required to create that final required result. Once they have built their own solution that does meet the required result, they then check their solution against the exam's proposed solution. By checking their conclusions against the exam's proposed solution and the givens offered in the question, they then can easily decide which required and optional results are achieved. If they know the material, they can answer the scenario questions—they just do it in a way others would call backwards!

It's important for candidates to see the forest *and* the trees and to know when to see each. In a question about a congested network, the candidate must decide whether the question is trying to ferret out the factual knowledge that FDDI is faster than 802.3 10 Mbps Ethernet or knowledge about the technical standards for installation and configuration details of FDDI. Candidates with extensive networking experience may be tempted to show off and choose the latter, when only the simple knowledge that FDDI is faster than Ethernet was required. Don't read information into the question that is not there!

Exam Interface Quirks—Sylvan Interface

The Sylvan exam interface has a peculiar quirk on long questions that can hurt you if you're not careful. This is particularly true if the testing center uses small monitors so that more questions are longer than one screen. On these long questions there is an elevator or scroll bar on the right side of the screen so that you can use the mouse to move down to read the remainder of the question.

When you reach the bottom of the question—but not until you reach the bottom—the left-hand selection box on the outside bottom of the screen changes from "More" to "Next." There is a built-in assumption that if you are not looking at the bottom of the screen when you select your answer, you've made a premature answer.

If you have moved back up the screen to reread the question, for example, and the very bottom of the screen is *not visible,* and you then check very near but not exactly on your answer, sometimes the box above your selection actually gets selected rather than the box you intended to check. To correct for this quirk, you should either be sure you are always looking at the very bottom of the screen before you select the answer or you should back up from the next question, by clicking on the "Previous" question box, to double-check your previous selection.

Select the Wrong Answers!

Okay, it sounds nuts. But the best advice around is to begin analysis of each question by selecting the answers that are clearly wrong. Every wrong answer eliminated gets you closer to the correct answer(s)! Often there are two answers that can be quickly eliminated, leaving you to focus your attention and time on fewer remaining options.

By carefully structuring your time, you can answer more questions correctly during the allotted exam period. Eliminate wrong and distracter answers first to narrow your attention to the more likely correct answers.

Indirect Questions

Microsoft exams are not straightforward. They often use questions that *indirectly* test your skill and knowledge, without coming straight out and asking you about the facts they are testing. For example, there is no exam question that actually asks, "Is the Windows NT 4.0 Emergency Repair Disk bootable?" and there is no question that says, "The Windows NT 4.0 Emergency Repair Disk is not bootable, True or False?" But you had better know that the Emergency Repair Disk (ERD) is *never* bootable. By knowing that the ERD cannot be booted, you can eliminate at least one wrong answer and therefore come closer to the right answer on one or more exams. *By the way, after you've once had an unfortunate experience that calls for actually using the Windows NT ERD, you'll never again have a doubt about whether you can boot to it—the ERD repair occurs considerably later, well after booting the computer.*

After you've taken a Microsoft exam or two, if you think you would be good at composing the kind of indirect question that tests many facets and levels at the same time, check out this URL, where you can get information about being a contract test writer for Microsoft:

Microsoft Certified Professional Web site—Become a Contract
Writer
http://www.microsoft.com/Train_Cert/Mcp/examinfo/iwrite.
htm

Simulation Questions

Some Microsoft exams make extensive use of a new type of question—*simulation questions*. Simulation questions provide the candidate with a working model of an administrative tool such as the Microsoft Management Console and require the candidate to perform a series of steps to accomplish a stated purpose or determine required information. One exam that makes extensive use of simulation questions is the IIS 4.0 exam.

Microsoft has an FAQ entitled, "Frequently Asked Questions about Exams with Simulations," at http://www.microsoft.com/mcp/articles/IISFAQ.htm that mentions a number of tips for scoring well on simulation questions, including

- Change only settings that apply directly to the solution of the problem.

- Assume default settings if you have not been provided with information you think you may need.

- If you type in an entry, make sure it is spelled correctly.

- Close the Microsoft Management Console simulation window after completing each simulation question.

Simulation questions make up a significant portion of some exams, but the bulk of the questions are still the traditional multiple-choice type of question.

Adaptive Testing

Traditional Microsoft exams are collections of 50 to 70 multiple choice questions. If you are uncertain about any questions, you can guess or leave them blank and then mark them for later reference. At the end of the exam you can go back and reconsider your marked questions.

Microsoft exams are gradually being migrated to a new format called *computer adaptive testing (CAT) exams*. In a CAT exam you start with an easy-to-moderate question. If you get it right, you are given a more difficult question next. If you get it wrong, you get an easier one. This process continues until a statistical algorithm calculates that it has determined your proficiency with the product according to predefined criteria.

The main differences with the newer CAT exams to the test-taker are

■ You are presented with fewer questions; typically, after 15 to 25 questions, the text engine reaches a decision about your level of proficiency.

■ This also means that CAT exams are shorter than traditional exams.

■ You can't mark a question and then go back to it later. You must answer every question, or you fail.

■ You don't get any feedback about what areas of the product (planning, management, troubleshooting, etc.) you scored poorly in. That's up to you to figure out.

Scheduling an Exam

Register by exam number. Say, "I want to register to take Microsoft exam number 70-058." Also know the exact title of the exam so that it's familiar when the test registrar reads it back to you.

The Microsoft MCSE exams are administered by or through VUE (Virtual University Enterprises, a division of National Computer Systems, Inc.) or Sylvan Prometric. Either Sylvan or VUE can provide MCSE testing. Both VUE and Sylvan have access to your records of previous MCSE tests, and both vendors report your test results directly to Microsoft. Taking an examination through either vendor organization does not obligate you to use the same organization or the same testing center for any other examination.

VUE began testing for Microsoft in May of 1998 after requests for another vendor from throughout the Microsoft professional community. VUE began by offering exams only in English and largely in North America. VUE projects significant growth during 1998 and 1999, with worldwide coverage available by June of 1999.

SYLVAN PROMETRIC

To schedule yourself for an exam through Sylvan, or for information about the Sylvan testing center nearest you, call 800-755-3926 (800-755-exam) or write to Sylvan at

Sylvan Prometric
Certification Registration
2601 88th Street West
Bloomington, MN 55431

To register online:

Sylvan Prometric (Nav1)
http://www.slspro.com/

Sylvan also offers 16 short sample online exams, called Assessment Tests, on various Microsoft products. (*Although Sylvan has offered online registration for several months, reports have continued that would-be exam candidates are unable to use the online registration, despite valiant attempts—good luck!*)
Phone: 800-755-3926

VIRTUAL UNIVERSITY ENTERPRISES

To schedule yourself for an exam through Virtual University Enterprises (VUE), or for information about the VUE testing center nearest you, call 888-837-8616 or visit VUE's Web site to register online 24 hours a day, 365 days a year:

Virtual University Enterprises (VUE)
5001 W 80th Street, Suite 401
Bloomington, MN 55437-1108

To register online:

http://www.vue.com/ms
North America: 888-837-8616 toll-free
612-897-7999

VUE is a new kid on the block, but never fear, its people are seasoned test people, and their promise to the industry has been new thinking in technology and service and higher levels of candidate and testing center service. VUE has a "we try harder" attitude and backs it up with higher standards for testing centers (800 × 600 video resolution on Windows 95 machines) and an agile new 32-bit testing engine. While VUE is in expansion mode, you should expect some growing pains, but also watch for some new thinking and professional amiability.

For instance, VUE immediately found a way to offer live online 24-hour, 7-days-a-week exam scheduling and rescheduling of Microsoft exams for busy professionals. And VUE offers on-site exam scheduling and rescheduling *at testing centers*. These conveniences will be tremendously valuable to individual candidates. Because VUE's operation is based on heavy Internet bandwidth, they are able to use secure Java-based system management and site administration software to handle all testing and services. Also, VUE delivers exams quickly to testing centers over the Internet rather than by modem and telephone lines, as Sylvan does.

When You Arrive at the Testing Center

Arrive early. It can put you at ease to check in 30 to 60 minutes early. Relax a bit before you actually sit for the exam. Some exam centers won't complete your check-in until the last minute before your scheduled time, and others will get you all signed up and then tell you to "let them know" when you're ready to begin. Sometimes they'll offer to let you begin "early." Starting a little bit late is also sometimes tolerated, if you want to review your notes one more time—be sure to ask first.

To check in, you'll be asked to provide proof of your identity. Two pieces of ID with your name and signature are required, one must have a photograph of you—a driver's license or passport and a credit card are adequate. There are testing center rules you'll be asked to read, sign, and date. Microsoft also has begun to require, on all new exams, that the candidate agree to a nondisclosure statement, discussed in the next section.

Testing center staff will explain their procedures and show you to the testing computers. This is the time to ask any questions about the testing rules. Find out, for instance, if you'll be allowed to leave the exam room to visit the restroom (with the *clock still running* on your exam) if your physical comfort demands a break.

CARRY WATER ONLY

Some folks bring bottled water, vitamins, or medications into the exam room, for their own comfort. You should consider what will make you most productive during the 90 minutes of your exam, and prepare accordingly.

Of course, the downside to drinking soda, coffee, or water during or even before the exam occurs later, when you are nearing the end of the 90-minute exam and really need to visit the restroom.

WRITING MATERIAL IN THE EXAM ROOM

This is a touchy area. Testing centers are required to be very picky about *cheat notes* carried *into or out of* the exam. There is a story of a candidate who had an ordinary napkin wrapped around a can of soda in the exam room and carried it out for disposal at the end of the exam. She was challenged about the napkin and probably would have been disqualified or worse had the napkin contained any writing.

Always ask for writing implements. Paper and pen are easier to use, but some testing centers will not allow them. Those centers which do not allow pen and paper will issue you marking pens and plasticized writing cards that are hard to use.

The marking pens commonly have a wide tip that makes writing difficult, and they dry out very quickly between uses if they will write at all—you must remember to replace the cap, or the pen will refuse to write the next time you try. Get the finest-tipped pens available. The tips seem to widen with use, so newer pens are better. Ask the testing center to open a *new* package of pens, and ask for two or three pens in case they go completely dry.

Also ask for another sheet or two of the $8\frac{1}{2}$ by 10 in plasticized writing material. If you have a large network drawing in mind, for instance, use the back of the card—2 in of the card's front are already in use by Sylvan Prometric. Don't force yourself to try to use those awkward marking pens in a small space—start another side or another sheet!

> **TEST TIP**
> Don't waste your precious exam time writing down any memorized notes on the exam room writing material. Write down any memorized notes during the time *before the exam* you could use for taking the how-to-use-this-exam-software tutorial (discussed next). Some exams call for more memorization than others, and some exams have a tremendous amount of minute detail. Use your time wisely by recording any easily forgotten formulas, rules of thumb, and mnemonics *before* you begin the exam, *after* you enter the exam room.
>
> The day before the exam, practice writing down all those notes you've decided will help you on your exam. Force yourself to write from memory only, to prove you can remember it long enough to write it down in the exam room.

ONLINE TUTORIAL

An optional exam tutorial is available before each MCSE exam. The tutorial is designed to show you how the computer-administered exam software works and to help you become familiar with how the exam will proceed *before the clock starts on your real exam.* Don't become confused by the presence of the tutorial—if the clock in the upper right corner is ticking, you are taking the real exam, not the tutorial!

 TEST TIP

If you happen to be nervous before an exam, it might help reduce your anxiety to take some off-the-clock time with the optional tutorial to breathe deeply and calm yourself down and get into the right mood for passing the exam. Even if you've already seen the tutorial and know exactly how to run the exam software, the tutorial can be a safety valve to give you a little time to adjust your attitude. Controlling your own use of time around the exam can give you just the boost you need!

REQUIRED NONDISCLOSURE AGREEMENT

Microsoft requires certification candidates to accept a nondisclosure agreement before taking some exams. If you take an exam that was first released after February 1998, you'll be required to provide an affirmation that you accept the terms of a brief, formal nondisclosure agreement. This policy eventually will cover all MCSE exams. Microsoft says that this policy will help maintain the integrity of the MCP program. The text of the agreement is provided in the sidebar and is also available at this URL:

Microsoft Certified Professional Web site—Certification Non-Disclosure Agreement for MCP Exams
http://www.microsoft.com/mcp/articles/nda.htm

NONDISCLOSURE AGREEMENT AND GENERAL TERMS OF USE FOR EXAMS DEVELOPED FOR THE MICROSOFT CERTIFIED PROFESSIONAL PROGRAM

This exam is Microsoft confidential and is protected by trade secret law. It is made available to you, the examinee, solely for the purpose of becoming certified in the technical area referenced in the title of this exam. You are expressly prohibited from disclosing, publishing, reproducing, or transmitting this exam, in whole or in part, in any form or by any means, verbal or written, electronic or mechanical, for any purpose, without the prior express written permission of Microsoft Corporation.

Click the Yes button to symbolize your signature and to accept these terms. Click the No button if you do not accept these terms. You must click Yes to continue with the exam.

MANDATORY DEMOGRAPHIC SURVEY

Microsoft says that it appreciates your participation in the mandatory demographic survey before each exam. For years, the survey was optional—now it is mandatory. Microsoft estimates that the survey will take most candidates less than 5 minutes. Of course, the survey time does not count against your clocked exam period.

To motivate you to furnish sincere and valid answers on the mandatory survey, Microsoft stresses that the survey results are vital to the program and useful for setting the passing score of each exam, validating new exam questions, and developing training materials for MCSE candidates. Microsoft says, "By providing accurate and complete information on this survey, you will help Microsoft improve both the quality of MCP exams and the value of your certification."

The mandatory demographic survey collects information, keyed to your Social Security Number, about your work experience, your work environment, the software tested by the exam, and information about your exam preparation methods. The survey has three components. One portion is common to all exams, another is keyed to the exam track, and the third portion is specific to that one exam. Carefully note the wording of any promises of confidentiality, data cross-matching, or disclosure of your personal information.

CHECK THE EXAM NUMBER AND EXAM TITLE

Although it is unlikely, there have been stories about the wrong test being loaded for an exam candidate. The first task of taking a Microsoft exam is to be sure you are beginning the exam *you intended to take.* By double-checking the exam number and exam title, you might save yourself and the testing center hours of difficulty, if somehow the wrong exam showed up for you. Therefore, be sure you check the exam title before you begin the clock on the exam—checking the exam title doesn't need to be part of your timed exam.

ITEM REVIEW STRATEGIES

If your exam is of the traditional type and *not* an adaptive test, in the upper right-hand corner there is a small square box with the word "Mark" next to it. This little box is your key to another method to better manage your time during MCSE exams. When you encounter a question that stumps you or leaves you feeling like you didn't study the right material *at all*, check an answer with the best guess you can quickly make, check the "Mark" box, and move on to the next question. At the end of the exam there is an item review option that will allow you to revisit only the questions you marked!

When you reach the end of the questions, a page that summarizes your answers to all the questions is shown. It has red marks where you have not yet completed the question or skipped it entirely. Try to fill in at least a best guess as you go through the exam the first time—you can't get a question right that was left blank or incomplete!

The end-of-exam summary page also shows which items you marked for later review. If you click on the box for item review, you will be taken back through your marked questions from the beginning of the exam, without needing to see the other, non-marked questions intervening. Or if you double-click on any answer on the summary page, you'll be taken to that question, marked or not.

After you're quite comfortable with the testing process, you might want to consider this advanced strategy for dealing with marked questions. As you go through the exam, remember to jot down topics that are in the "stumper" questions you've marked. Then, if a later question includes that same topic, make a note of what the question number is, right next to your "tough topics" list. This way, when it comes time for you to review the questions you marked, you'll have the numbers of informative or "clue-filled" questions to review on that same topic. Although the final summary screen allows you to access any question, unless you recorded the question numbers as you went along, it may be too time consuming to find the informative questions during item review.

SOURCES OF ADDITIONAL INFORMATION

Microsoft maintains a large staff to handle your questions about the MCSE certificate. Give them a call at

Microsoft MCP Program: 800-636-7544

If you have a CompuServe account, you can access the Microsoft area with this command:

```
GO MSEDCERT
```

Microsoft Newsgroups

By pointing your Internet news-reading software to the NNTP news server at Microsoft, you can read ongoing news, questions, answers, and comments on dozens of topics close to Microsoft products.

Microsoft Public NNTP server: msnews.microsoft.com

Two typical hierarchies for your attention are these:

```
microsoft.public.windowsnt
microsoft.public.inetexplorer
```

The Saluki E-mail Mailing List

Saluki is a very active majordomo Internet email mailing list. Some days have 50 to 100 messages about MCSE studies and related topics. In order to subscribe, send an email message to majordomo@saluki.com.

In the body of the message write:

```
subscribe mcse Yourfirstname Lastname
```

For example:

```
subscribe mcse Scott Armstrong
```

You may use an alias if you wish.

For further information about Saluki, write to Scott Armstrong at saluki@gate.net or Dean Klug at deano@gate.net.

Focus of this Book: Exam 70-081: Implementing and Supporting Microsoft Exchange Server 5.5

Exam Format

The Exchange 5.5 exam recently (November 1998) has been changed from traditional format to adaptive format. This means that you can expect approximately 15 to 25 questions, after which the exam engine will calculate your score. Generally, the better your proficiency with the product, the fewer the number of questions you are presented with.

Exam Preparation Guide

Your final authority for determining what you need to know to pass the Exchange 5.5 exam is the Exam Preparation Guide for Exam 70-081, which can be found on the Training and Certification Web site at

http://www.microsoft.com/mcp/exam/stat/SP70-081.htm

This guide outlines in detail the skills being measured by the exam and correlates these skills with the Microsoft official courses covering Exchange Server 5.5 (courses MS 973 and MS 869), available at Microsoft Certified Technical and Education Centers (CTECs), and also with the Microsoft self-paced training kit, *Microsoft Exchange Server 5.5 Training* (course MS 1040), available from Microsoft Press.

This *Accelerated MCSE Study Guide* was prepared from the Exchange 5.5 exam preparation guide and is designed to give you understanding of the concepts and practices of planning, installing, configuring, managing, and troubleshooting Exchange 5.5 implementations at the enterprise level. This study guide is not intended to replace sitting in a Microsoft official course or working through a Microsoft Press self-study kit on Exchange 5.5. Neither is it intended to replace dedicated hours of hands-on practice with the product itself. What this study guide does provide is an invaluable guide for preparing for the Exchange 5.5 exam which, combined with classroom or self-study plus product experience, will provide a solid base for exam success.

For Further Resources

Be sure to check out my Web site at

http://www.mtit.com

You will find there a list of additional resources to help you prepare for this exam, a list of errata for this book (if any errors are found), and other useful information.

Good luck!

CHAPTER 2

Planning and Implementation

This chapter provides an introduction to Microsoft Exchange Server 5.5 and its implementation as an enterprise-level messaging system. Topics covered include

- What is Exchange Server?
- Supported features and protocols
- How does Exchange Server work?
- Basic concepts and terminology
- Planning an Exchange implementation
- Client access licenses
- Installing Exchange Server
- Where do we go from here?
- For review

What Is Exchange Server?

Microsoft Exchange Server is an enterprise-level, client/server messaging system that meets all your company's messaging and groupware needs. Combined together with its powerful clients,

Microsoft Outlook and *Microsoft Outlook Express,* users can

- Send messages together with documents, graphics, and other attachments to other users in their organization and to other mail systems, including the Internet
- Create public folders for posting documents and collaborating with other users
- Connect to other users' calendars for making appointments and scheduling meetings
- Keep track of contacts, prioritize tasks, and track events in their journals
- Access their mail remotely over the Internet using a standard Web browser

 TIP

Although most of this book (and Microsoft Exam 70-081) deals with configuring and managing Exchange Server, you will need to be familiar with Exchange clients as well, and coverage of these clients is included in this book.

Supported Features and Protocols

Some of the important features of Microsoft Exchange Server include

- *Interoperability.* Exchange provides a complete stand-alone messaging solution for companies of all sizes, but the reality is that many large companies already have existing mail systems such as Microsoft Mail 3.x, Lotus cc:Mail and Lotus notes, IBM PROFS and SNADS, standard X.400 mail systems, or standard Internet SMTP mail systems. Exchange includes *connectors* for all the preceding mail systems so that companies can integrate Exchange into their existing mail systems. Third-party connectors and gateways can be added for interoperability with any other messaging system.
- *Migration.* Large companies with several incompatible mail systems incur large costs supporting their various mail systems. Exchange includes migration tools for moving users from existing mail systems to Exchange, enabling companies to integrate

their various existing mail systems into a single, unified mail system that meets all their messaging needs and reduces their support costs.

- *Internet.* Exchange supports all the important Internet standards for messaging, including SMTP, POP3, and IMAP4 protocols. Exchange also supports access to users' mailboxes through HTTP using standard Web browsers and can host USENET-style NNTP newsgroups. Finally, Exchange supports LDAP for client access to the Exchange directory services.

- *Clients.* Exchange supports clients for all major operating systems, including MS-DOS, all versions of Microsoft Windows, Apple Macintosh, OS/2, and UNIX operating systems.

- *Reliability.* Exchange includes fault-tolerant directory services and message stores and can intelligently reroute messages when a messaging link fails. Servers and messaging links can be monitored, and alerts can be sent to administrators when a server or link is down. The size of the message store depends only on the capabilities of your hardware. Support for Microsoft Cluster Server is included to provide additional fault tolerance in case of hardware failure.

- *Security.* Exchange supports encrypted e-mail through standard X.509 digital certificates, Secure MIME (S/MIME) encrypted message encoding, and Secure Sockets Layer (SSL) protocol. Exchange can use Microsoft Certificate Server as a Certificate Authority (CA) and includes Key Management (KM) server for administering security for users in your organization. Multiple address containers can be created within the Global Address List so that you can host several companies on one Exchange system, each with its own virtual Exchange organization.

- *Chat and NetMeeting.* Exchange includes an Internet Chat service for letting users communicate in real time, and supports Microsoft NetMeeting users by allowing them to perform Internet Locator Server (ILS) lookups using the Exchange directory service.

How Does Exchange Server Work?

Exchange is a *client/server mail system,* which means that the job of messaging is split between the client (e.g., Microsoft Outlook) and the server (Microsoft Exchange Server). Communication between a client and an Exchange server takes place using remote procedure calls (RPCs). A *remote procedure call* is a communication mechanism whereby an application on one computer makes a call to execute a function within an application on another computer. For example, if user A sends a message to user B, then

- User A's Outlook program connects to the Exchange server using RPCs and transfers the message to the server.

- The server processes the message, determines that the recipient is user B, and moves the message into user B's mailbox on the server.

- The server then connects to user B's Outlook program using RPCs and notifies Outlook that there is a new message waiting, and the new message is transferred to user B's Inbox in their Outlook program.

This client/server approach is more effective than the shared-file mail system approach of older mail programs such as Microsoft Mail. In *shared-file mail systems,* the mail server acts as a passive post office that the client regularly polls, effectively asking, "Is there new mail for me yet?" This puts greater processing demand on the client and increases the overall level of traffic on the network.

Basic Concepts and Terminology

One of the main difficulties in becoming familiar with implementing and administering Exchange as a mail system is language. There are a number of concepts and terms that have to be learned first before you can understand how to plan an Exchange implementation for a company (or just pass the exam). Here is a brief summary of some of the more important new terms, more or less in the order in which you have to consider them when planning to implement Exchange:

- *Organization.* An organization represents all the Exchange sites and servers in a company. The name of your organization is usually the same as your company name.

- *Site.* A collection of one or more Exchange servers that are connected by permanent, high-speed network connections. These could be LAN connections (10 or 100 Mbps or faster) or dedicated WAN links (a T-1 line). The critical thing is that the underlying transport mechanism must support RPCs. Sites generally are managed as a unit and represent some geographic grouping, e.g., cities, states, or countries, depending on the scope of your enterprise.

- *Server.* A single Exchange server within a site. Servers are used for storing messages and public folders, for routing messages to other servers, and for administering all aspects of the organization. Servers can have general-purpose messaging functions or can be tuned to perform a specific function only (e.g., routing mail to another site or hosting public folder content). Each Exchange server has four core components, which are each implemented as Windows NT services:

  1. *Directory Service.* Acts as a kind of central telephone book for keeping track of all users, sites, and servers and their properties.
  2. *Information Store.* A database containing users' mailboxes and their messages (*Private Information Store*) or public folders and their postings (*Public Information Store*).
  3. *Message Transfer Agent (MTA).* Responsible for seeing that messages are routed (delivered) between servers, sites, and remote mail systems.
  4. *System Attendant.* A maintenance service that must always be running and provides logging, monitoring, and other administrative functions.

- *Service Account.* Windows NT services need to run in the security context of a Windows NT account. Since the built-in system account is local to each server, whereas Exchange services need to interact remotely with each other, each Exchange site requires the use of a Windows NT account called the *Exchange Service Account.* This is the account that will be used to run Exchange services on each server and to allow Exchange services on different servers to interact with each other. Create this account prior to installing the first Exchange server in your site. You can call it anything you like (e.g., ExchangeService) and should assign it a secure password. The service account does not need to be an administrator account.

> **TIP**
>
> If you change the password of the site service account using User Manager for Domains, you also need to change it on the Site Configuration container's property sheet or Exchange services will fail to start for servers in your site.

- *Directory.* The database of all information about the organization, including its sites, servers, connectors, and recipients. This is a distributed database; i.e., it is replicated between Exchange servers so that each server contains a copy of the organization's entire directory database. Replication takes place in several ways:

  1. *Directory synchronization.* Servers in the same site exchange directory information with each other using directory synchronization. This happens automatically every 5 minutes and does not need to be configured in any way.
  2. *Directory replication.* Sites exchange directory information with each other using directory replication. This process requires that a connector first be used to establish messaging connectivity between the sites. Since sites may be connected by either dedicated or dial-up links, directory replication can be configured and scheduled.

- *Recipient.* Anyone or anything that can receive a message. This includes

  1. *Mailbox.* Stores messages for someone in your company who has a Windows NT user account. A user's mailbox is stored on his or her home server, which is specified when the mailbox is created.
  2. *Custom recipient.* Someone on another mail system, e.g., the Internet email address of someone your users frequently send messages to. Custom recipients are listed in the global address list for the organization, but they don't have mailboxes on the system.
  3. *Distribution list (DL).* A mailing list for mass mailings to multiple recipients simultaneously.
  4. *Public folder.* A place where any user can post a message or document so that others can view or modify it. Used for sharing ideas and collaborating on projects.
  5. *Mailbox agent.* A Windows NT service that receives messages instead of an actual user. The *Schedule+ Free/Busy Connector*

is an example of a mailbox agent that receives messages from Outlook clients about their free and busy times for making appointments and scheduling meetings.

- *Global Address List.* A list that contains all recipients in your organization. You can create subsets of this list called *address book views* that show users by location, department, or some other attribute.

- *Connector.* A Windows NT service that enables messages to be routed to another site in your organization or to a remote mail system, which could be either another Exchange organization or a foreign mail system (SMTP, X.400, Lotus cc:Mail, or any mail system other than Exchange). There are several different kinds of connectors, depending on whether you want to connect to another site in your organization, the Internet, or some other remote mail system.

- *Bridgehead Server.* An Exchange server in your site that acts as a kind of funnel for handling all messages sent through a specific connector.

- *Gateway.* Similar to a connector, a gateway translates messages from one format to another and routes them to a foreign mail system.

- *Server Monitor.* A tool for monitoring the health of the servers in your organization. An alert can be triggered or a message sent if one of your servers runs into difficulty.

- *Link Monitor.* A tool for monitoring the health of connectors between sites and other mail systems. Again, an alert or message can be generated if messages cannot be routed through one of your connectors.

There are other concepts and terms that are important to learn in order to fully understand Exchange, but these will be dealt with as they occur throughout the book.

Planning an Exchange Implementation

A whole lot of thinking needs to be done before you try to implement Exchange as a messaging solution for your company. Planning is essential, because some things, once done, cannot be undone easily without reinstalling Exchange on your servers. Here are some of the things you need to plan for before implementing Exchange:

Organization

Decide on your organization name ahead of time. If you want to change it later, you will have to reinstall Exchange on every server in your organization! Your organization name is typically your company's name, e.g., SampleCorp

User Needs

The needs of your users are paramount in planning an Exchange implementation. Users' needs determine where you install your servers, what services and connectors are installed on the servers, where public folders are located, and so on. Table 2-1 shows some possible needs of users and how you can meet those needs.

Sites

Exchange servers are grouped together into sites, which usually represent geographic locations such as cities, states, countries, or even continents, depending on the scope of your enterprise.

Table 2-1 Examples of Users' Needs and How to Meet Them

Users' Needs	How to Meet Their Needs
Email connectivity to the Internet	Install the Internet Mail Service
Remote access to mail	Install Windows NT RAS
Interoperability with existing Lotus cc:Mail system	Install cc:Mail Connector
Verification of identity and confidentiality	Use digital certificates
Access USENET newsgroups	Create a Newsfeed
Enable mass mailings to departments	Create distribution lists
Facilitate addressing within departments	Create address book views
Enable users to remotely access their mail using a Web browser	Install Outlook Web Access

When planning your sites, some of the things you need to consider include

- *Site names.* These are generally geographic (e.g., Vancouver) or the names of subsidiaries. Determining the boundaries of your sites is an important first step in planning your Exchange implementation.

- *Connectivity.* Exchange servers within a site need to be connected by high-speed permanent network connections that support RPCs. Typically, this means LAN connections using TCP/IP. If some of the servers in your site are connected to the rest using a slow connection, consider placing them in a different site.

- *Network bandwidth.* If your messaging and public folder access traffic is high, you may use dedicated high-speed connections between sites like T-1 or T-3 lines and install the Site Connector on selected Exchange servers to enable intersite messaging. However, if intersite traffic is low, you may be able to get away with dial-up connections between sites using Windows NT RAS and the Dynamic RAS Connector to join sites together.

- *Security context.* All Exchange servers within the same site must use the same Exchange service account. This typically means either that Exchange servers in your site belong to the same Windows NT domain or that some belong to one domain and others belong to *trusted* domains.

- *Directory replication.* Exchange servers within a site synchronize their directory databases automatically and frequently. If you would like to schedule how often servers replicate their directory information, place them in different sites.

- *Users.* Users' home servers (the Exchange server where their mailbox resides) should be on their local LAN connection to prevent excessive intersite and WAN traffic. Another consideration is that users who frequently send mail to each other (e.g., users in the same department) should be on the same LAN.

- *Foreign connectivity.* You will need to install connectors for the foreign mail systems to which you need to connect your organization. For example, you could install the Internet Mail Service on selected Exchange servers to allow users in your organization to send and receive messages to and from the Internet.

- *Fault tolerance.* Connectivity between sites can be made fault tolerant by establishing redundant connections. For example, two sites connected by a T-1 line could be joined using a Site Connector, and a backup dial-up ISDN link could be established using a Dynamic RAS Connector in case the T-1 link goes down.

- *Message size limits.* You can control intersite messaging traffic by limiting the size of messages sent, but you can't limit the number of messages users send.

Servers

When planning your individual Exchange servers, you will need to consider a number of factors:

- *Server name.* The name of an Exchange server is by default its Windows NT name. Plan your server names carefully—if you want to change a server's name, you need to remove it from the site, rename it, and reinstall Exchange!

- *Server role.* Exchange servers can be configured for particular roles to optimize performance and messaging traffic in your organization. The more roles a server has to play, the greater its hardware requirements will be. Some common roles for Exchange servers might be one or more of the following:

  - *Dedicated home server.* Delete the public information store, and don't install any connectors. Dedicated home servers make mailboxes easier to back up.
  - *Dedicated public folder server.* Delete the private information store, and don't install any connectors. Dedicated public folder servers make public folders easier to back up.
  - *Expansion server.* When a user sends a message to a distribution list (DL), the list must first be expanded into its individual recipients before the message can be sent. If your organization makes heavy use of DLs, you can dedicate one server to the job of expanding the DLs. This server should have a powerful CPU.
  - *Bridgehead server.* Install a connector to establish directory replication with another site or messaging connectivity with another site or mail system. If you don't create mailboxes or host public folders, then your server will be a dedicated bridgehead server. You can delete the private or public information store on a server, but not both.
  - *Directory synchronization server.* Install a Dirsync Server or Dirsync Requestor to establish directory synchronization

with Microsoft Mail systems or any foreign mail system using the MS Mail directory synchronization protocol.

- *Key Management server.* Install the Key Management component to enable advanced security for your users. Only one KM server should be installed in your organization.

In addition, some of your Exchange servers may have other roles, including Windows NT domain controllers, Windows NT RAS servers, IIS Web servers, and so on.

- *Server resources.* One key planning issue is to ensure that Exchange servers have sufficient hard disk resources to handle the expected size and anticipated growth of the private and public information stores. In addition, you may want to limit the amount of disk space used by establishing policies that

  - Set storage limits on the maximum size of mailboxes and public folders.
  - Set expiration policies on how long content can remain in mailboxes and public folders.
  - Limit the maximum size of messages sent.

Naming Conventions

In addition to giving names to your organization, sites, and servers, you also need to decide how to name mailboxes and generate e-mail aliases. Each object in the Exchange directory database generally has two kinds of names:

- A *display name,* the visible name for a directory object when viewed using the Exchange Administrator program and when the address book is viewed using a client such as Microsoft Outlook. This always can be modified by the administrator.

- A *directory name,* the internal name of the object in the directory database. This can be modified by the administrator, with the caveat that the directory names for organizations, sites, and servers cannot be changed.

Note that it is the directory name of a mailbox that is used to generate the email alias for the user. For example, if you create a mailbox called Sam Smith using the Exchange Administrator program, Exchange will use SamS as the directory name and email alias, so the user's SMTP address might be

SamS@Vancouver.SampleCorp.com

By default, the email alias is composed of the first name with the first initial of the last name appended to it. You can change this naming convention by selecting Options from the Tools menu in the Exchange Administrator program.

DIRECTORY NAMES

Every site, server, connector, mailbox, or other item in Exchange is associated with an object in the Exchange directory database. This database is hierarchical in structure, and objects within it have unique names called *distinguished names* (DNs) that are of the general form

```
o = organization/ou = site/cn = ...[/cn = ...[/cn = ...]]
```

where o = **name of organization**
       ou = **organizational unit, i.e., name of site**
       cn = **common name, i.e., the next level(s) of the database hierarchy**

For example, a mailbox for user Bob Jones whose home server is in the Toronto site of organization SampleCorp would have the distinguished name

```
o = SampleCorp/ou = Toronto/cn = Recipients/cn = BobJ
```

since his mailbox (BobJ) is located in the Recipients container for the Toronto site.

Client Access Licenses

Before you install Exchange Server, you need to be aware of licensing issues so that you will be fully compliant with all licensing requirements. Because Exchange Server is one of the Microsoft BackOffice series of products, you will need to purchase one *client access license* (CAL) for each user who will be connecting Exchange servers in your organization to access their mailbox, regardless of how they connect. For example, if you have 300 local users in your organization and 50 remote users, with their mailboxes distributed among several Exchange sites and servers, you will need to purchase 350 CALs. For legal information on Microsoft licensing requirements, and to make sure you are fully in compliance with these requirements, contact Microsoft.

Installing Exchange Server

Once you have planned the layout and configuration of your Exchange organization, it's time to install your Exchange servers. Follow these general procedures:

Create an Exchange Service Account

You can create one service account for each site, as described earlier. If you have permanent high-speed connections between your sites, then you can use one service account for your entire organization.

Meet the Hardware Requirements

Table 2-2 shows the minimum and recommended hardware requirements for installing Exchange.

Meet the Software Requirements

Exchange Server computers require the following software:

- Windows NT Server 4.0 or later

Table 2-2 Minimum and Recommended Hardware Requirements for Exchange Server

Resource	Minimum	Recommended
Processor	Pentium 90	Pentium 166 or higher
RAM	24 MB	32 MB or higher
Disk subsystem	250 MB	■ One physical disk for operating system and pagefile ■ Mirror set for transaction log files ■ Stripe set for all other Exchange components

- Windows NT Service Pack 3 or later
- TCP/IP protocol if connecting to the Internet
- If you plan to use Outlook Web Access to provide users with access to their email through a standard Web browser, then you will need Internet Information Server (IIS) version 3 or higher with Active Server Pages (ASP) installed on a server. This server does not need to be an Exchange server.
- If you plan to use Key Management (KM) server for advanced security, you will need Internet Information Server version 4 (IIS 4.0) with Microsoft Certificate Server installed on a server. This server does not need to be an Exchange server.
- If you plan to use Microsoft Cluster Server to provide fault tolerance, you need to use Windows NT Server Enterprise Edition 4.0.
- If you plan to use the MS Mail Connector to establish messaging connectivity with MS Mail for AppleTalk Networks (a.k.a. QuarterDeck Mail) mail systems, then the server with the connector must be running Windows NT Services for Macintosh.

Logon as Administrator

The administrator account you are logged on with when installing Exchange will be granted Permissions Admin role on the Exchange Server you are installing.

Install Exchange

Run the setup program and choose

- *Typical.* Installs Exchange Server and Exchange Administrator.
- *Complete/Custom.* Use to install connectors and other options in addition to the preceding.
- *Minimum.* Installs Exchange Server only.

If this is the first server in your site, you must specify the organization and site names by selecting Create a New Site. If your server will join an existing site, you must select Join an Existing Site and specify the name of a functioning Exchange server within that site.

If you are upgrading an earlier version of Exchange Server instead of installing a fresh version, the upgrade process is straightforward. Just make sure you first disable any server monitors that are monitoring that server's services. As an alternative to disabling them, you can put the monitors into *maintenance mode*. You also should do a full backup prior to upgrading the server. Considerations related to versions include

- Upgrading Exchange 5.0 to Exchange 5.5. This proceeds normally.

- Upgrading Exchange 4.0 to Exchange 5.5. First apply Exchange 4.0 Service Pack 2; then install Exchange 5.5, which first upgrades the server to Exchange 5.0 and then to Exchange 5.5.

Run Performance Optimizer

When Setup finishes, it prompts you to run the Exchange Performance Optimizer program. This wizard analyzes your memory and hard disk configuration in order to determine the best location for storing the information store database files, directory database files, transaction log files, and other Exchange components. It also determines how much RAM should be reserved for the various Exchange services. Make sure you run the Performance Optimizer now and after every major configuration change you make on the server, e.g., adding an additional drive or more memory, installing a connector, and so on.

Verifying Your Configuration

After Setup is complete and Performance Optimizer has run, use Services in Control Panel to verify that the following services are running:

- Microsoft Exchange Directory
- Microsoft Exchange Information Store
- Microsoft Exchange Message Transfer Agent
- Microsoft Exchange System Attendant

Then try starting the Exchange Administrator program and verify that your Exchange site and server objects are configured properly.

Where Do We Go from Here?

Depending on the role you planned for your new server, you now need to configure its services and install connectors or other components so that it can take its place in your Exchange organization. These tasks are taken up in the remainder of this book as each type of Exchange component is introduced and explained.

For Review

Here are a few general questions you can use to quiz yourself. If you are unsure how to answer a question or perform a task, go back and read through the relevant sections in this chapter again.

1. What must you install on an Exchange server to enable connectivity with a foreign mail system such as cc:Mail?

2. What are some Internet protocols supported by Exchange?

3. What kind of network connectivity must exist between all Exchange servers in a given site?

4. Name some possible roles for which Exchange servers can be configured.

5. Name and state the function of the four core components of Exchange Server. How are these components implemented?

6. What is the Exchange Service Account, and what is it used for?

7. Describe the two different ways in which directory information is replicated within an Exchange organization.

8. Name and describe the five different kinds of Exchange recipients.

9. A user opens the address book in Microsoft Outlook and sees a list of all 15,000 users in the Exchange organization. What should the administrator create in order to make it easier for users to use their address books?

10. Compare and contrast *server monitors* with *link monitors*.

11. Why is it important to carefully plan ahead of time the names of your Exchange organization, sites, and servers?

12. What component could you install on Exchange if remote users needed to access their mail using only a standard Web browser such as Internet Explorer?

13. What factors should be considered in deciding where to locate Exchange servers on your company network?

14. How can you manage the amount of space that is used by the hard drives on your Exchange servers?

15. What is the difference between a *display name* and a *directory name?*

16. What are the minimum and recommended hardware requirements for Exchange?

17. What are the software requirements for Exchange?

18. What does Performance Optimizer do, and when should you run it?

CHAPTER 3

Exchange Administrator

This chapter looks at the main GUI tool for administering Exchange servers, the *Exchange Administrator program*. Topics covered include

- Exchange tools
- The Exchange Administrator program
- Permissions and roles
- Where do we go from here?
- For review

Exchange Tools

Exchange includes a number of GUI-based and command-line tools and utilities for administering Exchange sites and servers. Additionally, a number of Windows NT administrative tools are also useful for administering Exchange.

GUI Tools

The GUI-based tools installed with Exchange include

■ *Exchange Administrator.* The primary tool for administering an Exchange organization, allowing you to manage its sites, servers, connectors, and recipients. Most of this book will deal with using Exchange Administrator to configure various aspects of your organization.

■ *Performance Optimizer.* A wizard that examines your current memory and disk subsystem configurations and suggests ways to optimize performance by relocating files and reallocating memory. You should run this tool when you make major configuration changes to your server, such as installing a connector or deleting the private information store. We will look at this tool in Chapter 10.

■ *Migration Wizard.* A tool for moving mailboxes and their content, address lists, and public folders from other mail systems to Exchange. We will look at this tool in Chapter 14.

Command-Line Tools

Command-line tools installed with Exchange are primarily for maintenance and troubleshooting and are discussed further in Chapter 13. These tools include

■ *Admin.exe.* This is actually the Exchange Administrator, which can be run from the command line to do various tasks. This is covered later in this chapter.

■ *Edbutil.exe.* This tool checks the integrity of the Exchange directory database and attempts to repair any problems found.

■ *Isinteg.exe.* The Information Store Integrity Checker is a diagnostic tool for checking and fixing the information store when problems occur.

■ *Mtacheck.exe.* This tool checks the internal database of the Message Transfer Agent (MTA) to look for corrupt messages that are blocking the queue. Use it for troubleshooting the MTA when it stops and can't be restarted.

Windows NT Tools

Windows NT administrative tools that are important for administering Exchange include

■ *User Manager for Domains.* Installing Exchange on a server installs an add-on to User Manager for Domains that lets you create an associated mailbox for a user when you create that user's Windows NT account. You also can select an existing account and open the properties of its associated mailbox (if there is one) to configure the mailbox settings.

- *Windows NT Backup.* Installing Exchange on a server installs a new version of this tool that simplifies backing up and restoring Exchange servers. You can selectively back up

  - All Exchange servers in your organization
  - All servers in selected sites
  - Specific servers in selected sites.

  In addition, for each server you can select to back up either or both of the following critical components:

  - Information store
  - Directory database

- *Performance Monitor.* Additional objects and counters are added for monitoring Exchange services and functions. A number of preconfigured Performance Monitor *workspace files* (*.pmw) are available from the Start menu after Exchange is installed on a server.

- *Event Viewer.* The Application Log should be examined whenever performance or messaging problems arise using Exchange.

- *Control Panel.* Use the Services utility to start, stop, and pause Exchange services and configure their startup settings.

- Other useful Windows NT utilities, especially for troubleshooting Internet connectivity problems, include *ping, netstat,* and *telnet.*

Microsoft Outlook

Finally, Microsoft Outlook 98, although it is the primary client program for Exchange, also should be considered an Exchange administrative tool. This is so because there are a few administrative tasks that can only be done by client software, such as creating a new public folder.

The Exchange Administrator Program

As mentioned in Chapter 2, all configuration information for Exchange sites, servers, connectors, recipients, services, and other components are stored in a hierarchical database called the *direc-*

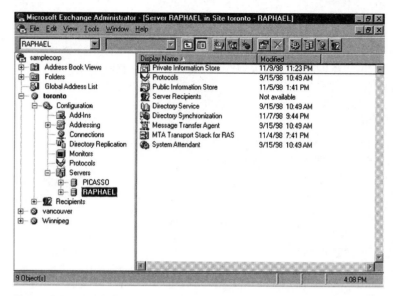

Figure 3-1 The Exchange Administrator program window showing the Exchange directory hierarchy.

tory database. This database is replicated to all Exchange servers in an organization to ensure fault tolerance and availability.

To view and configure objects in this directory hierarchy, you use the Exchange Administrator program (Fig. 3-1).

The Exchange Administrator window is divided into two window panes, similar to Windows Explorer. These two panes are

- *Container pane.* The left-hand pane shows all directory objects that are containers; i.e., they contain other objects.

- *Contents pane.* The right-hand pane shows all directory objects that are contained within the selected container object in the left-hand pane. These objects may be either *containers* (i.e., they contain additional objects) or *leaf objects* (i.e., they represent the end of a branch in the directory tree).

For example, in Figure 3-1 the Server container RAPHAEL is selected in the left-hand pane, and the right-hand pane shows the various directory objects contained by that container. Some of these objects in the right-hand pane are leaf objects, while others are containers themselves.

Taking a closer look at the directory hierarchy displayed in the container pane, we see that the root object in the hierarchy is the *Organization* container, in this example having the name SampleCorp. Directly beneath this root object, the second-level objects in the directory hierarchy include

- *Address Book Views.* These are subsets of the Global Address List object.

- *Folders.* These include Public Folders and System Folders objects.

- *Global Address List.* This is a list of all Recipient objects.

- *Sites.* Three Site containers are visible in the example: Toronto, Vancouver, and Winnipeg.

Inside the Site containers are third-level directory objects. For example, contained within the Site container Toronto are two more containers:

- *Configuration.* This container contains all the objects for configuring sites and their servers.

- *Recipients.* This container contains all the mailboxes, distribution lists, and other recipient objects created in the site.

We could go further: the third-level Servers container for Toronto contains two fourth-level Server containers PICASSO and RAPHAEL; these contain fifth-level objects such as Private Information Store, Protocols, and so on. Eventually, we reach the end of the line, with leaf objects at the tips of the tree's branches.

One important thing to know is that permissions flow naturally down the directory hierarchy. For example, if we assign user MaryS the *Permissions Admin* role on a site's Configuration container, these permissions flow into all objects contained within the container. Permissions are further discussed later in this chapter.

Installing Exchange Administrator

Exchange Administrator is installed on an Exchange server automatically when Setup is run in *Typical* mode, but you don't need to install it on every Exchange server in your organization. You also can use the *Complete/Custom* setup mode to install Exchange Administrator on a Windows NT Server or Workstation and use it to remotely administer to any Exchange servers in your site or organization with which you have RPC connectivity.

NOTE

You can install the Exchange Administrator program on a Windows NT Server or Workstation, but you cannot install it on Windows 95/98 or Windows 3.x

When you first start the Exchange Administrator, you must select an Exchange server to connect to for obtaining the necessary directory information to display the Exchange directory hierarchy. You also can use Connect to Server from the File menu to open multiple windows in Exchange Administrator, each based on a connection to a different server. Note that if directory replication is not up to date in your organization, the objects displayed in each window could be different.

Using Exchange Administrator

You can select any object (container or leaf) in either pane and click the Properties button on the toolbar (or press ALT + ENTER, or select Properties from the File menu) to open the *property sheet* for that object. For example, Figure 3-2 shows the property sheet for the Server container RAPHAEL selected in Figure 3-1.

This typical property sheet consists of a number of tabs, each of which contain various controls (listboxes, checkboxes, option buttons, etc.) for configuring the properties of the directory object. What makes Exchange such a difficult product to get your head around is the vast number and large variety of these property sheets!

You also can use the Exchange Administrator menu to perform a number of common administrative tasks, including

- Creating and configuring new recipients
- Installing and configuring connectors, MTA transport stacks, monitors, information stores, newsfeeds, and other Exchange components and services
- Exporting and importing information about recipients
- Extracting lists of user accounts from Windows NT and NetWare servers

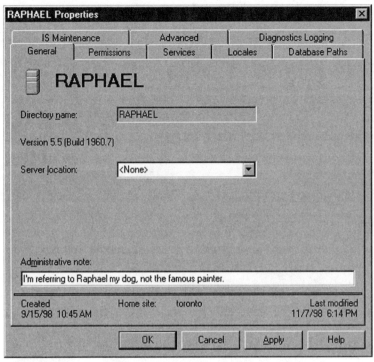

Figure 3-2   The property sheet for the Server container RAPHAEL, an example of an Exchange directory object's property sheet.

- Starting and stopping Server and Link Monitors
- Opening the Message Tracking Center to troubleshoot messaging problems
- Viewing newsgroup hierarchies
- Changing views and columns displayed in the contents pane

These tasks will be covered in later chapters in the context of their related topics.

TIP

It's important that you become familiar with the Exchange Administrator program, since the Preparation Guide for Exam 70-081 indicates that the exam may contain simulation items.

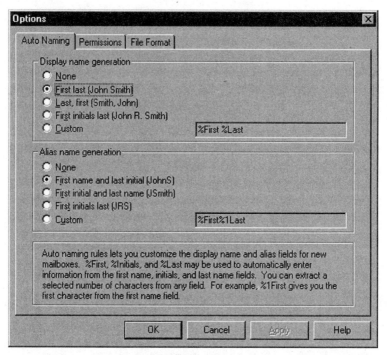

Figure 3-3   Configuring options for the Exchange Administrator program.

Configuring Exchange Administrator Options

Using Options from the Tools menu opens the Options dialog box (Fig. 3-3). The three tabs of this property sheet have the following uses:

- *Auto Naming.* This feature allows you to specify how the display name and email alias name are automatically generated when you create a new mailbox, e.g., SusanJ, Sjones, SJ, and so on.

- *Permissions.* This tab lets you choose whether to hide or show the Permissions tab when a directory object's property sheet is displayed and how information on that tab is displayed.

- *File Format.* This tab is used to configure the format of text files for the Directory Import and Directory Export processes.

Permissions and Roles

Exchange permissions are not the same as Windows NT permissions. Exchange permissions are used to grant different levels of

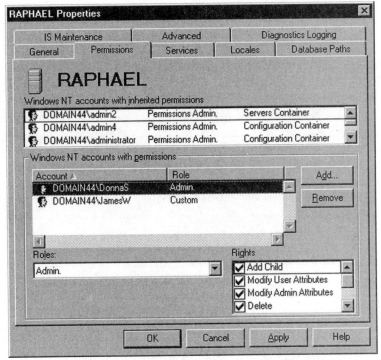

Figure 3-4   The Permissions tab for the Server container RAPHAEL.

access to the Exchange directory database, the information store, and other Exchange components and services.

The way it works is like this: Exchange permissions consist of a number of *rights* that are grouped together into *roles*. For each object in the directory hierarchy, a user's Windows NT account can be granted access to that object by assigning the user a specific role on that object's Permissions page. As an example, Figure 3-4 shows the Permissions page for the Server container RAPHAEL described earlier.

> **NOTE**
> If the objects in the directory hierarchy don't have a Permissions tab, use Options from the Tools menu to make this tab visible.

In the example in Figure 3-4, the top listbox shows which Windows NT accounts have permissions on the Server container

RAPHAEL by *inheritance,* i.e., by having permissions on a *parent container* of RAPHAEL. We can see, for example, that the account Admin2 has the Permissions Admin role on the parent Servers container (see Fig. 3-1 again, and note that the Server container RAPHAEL is contained within the Servers container).

The middle listbox shows those Windows NT accounts which have been explicitly granted permissions on RAPHAEL. For example, we can see that DonnaS has been explicitly granted the Admin role on RAPHAEL. You grant explicit rights to a user by using the Add button.

Finally, because DonnaS is selected in the middle listbox, we see her role (Admin) in the bottom-left listbox, while the bottom-right listbox shows her rights associated with that role. If you selectively add or remove any of these rights, her role would become a Custom role, which was done for the account JamesW.

Table 3-1 Exchange Rights

Right	Type of Permission Granted
Add child	Can create objects within a container
Modify user attribute	Can modify user-level attributes of an object
Modify admin attributes	Can modify administrator-level attributes of an object
Modify permissions	Can modify the permissions on the object
Delete	Can delete the object
Logon	Can access the directory database*
Replication	Can replicate directory information*
Mailbox owner	Can read and delete messages in the mailbox
Search	Can view the contents of the container
Send as	Can send a message using the sender's return address

*Needed by the Exchange service account

Table 3-1 summarizes the individual *rights* that can be selectively assigned or withheld from a user. You should be aware that not all these rights may be available for a particular directory object.

In order to simplify assigning permissions to users on directory objects, the rights listed in Table 3-1 are consolidated into a number of built-in collections of rights called *roles*. These roles are listed in Table 3-2 along with their associated rights. Note that not all roles can be assigned to users for any given directory object.

One common reason for assigning permissions is when you want to grant another Windows NT administrator account permission to use the Exchange Administrator program for administering a site in your organization. To do this, you need to grant

Table 3-2 Exchange Roles

			Role				
Right	**Admin**	**Per-missions Admin**	**Service Account Admin**	**View Only Admin**	**User**	**Send As**	**Search**
Add child	√	√	√				
Modify user attributes	√	√	√		√		√
Modify admin attributes	√	√		√			
Delete	√	√		√			
Logon	√	√	√	√			
Modify permission		√	√				
Replication			√				
Mailbox owner			√		√		
Send as			√		√	√	
Search							√

the account the Permissions Admin role on both the Site container and its Configuration container. All other objects within the site will then inherit these permissions by default.

Alternatively, if you only wanted to give an administrator fewer privileges so that he or she could create new mailboxes for any server in the site but couldn't change site configuration parameters, you would grant that administrator the Permissions Admin role on the Site container but the View Only Admin role on the Configuration container.

Where Do We Go from Here?

Now that we know how to use the Exchange Administrator program to view the directory hierarchy, we will next look at how to use this program to configure the basic properties of Exchange *sites*.

For Review

Here are a few general questions you can use to quiz yourself. If you are unsure how to answer a question or perform a task, go back and read through the relevant sections in this chapter again.

1. Name and describe the function of the various GUI, command-line, and Windows NT administrative tools used for administering Exchange servers.
2. Describe the difference between *containers* and *leaf objects*.
3. Draw a sketch showing some of the major objects in the directory hierarchy of a typical Exchange organization.
4. How could you install only the Exchange Administrator program on a Windows NT Workstation computer?
5. What are some of the common administrative tasks you can perform using the Exchange Administrator menu?
6. How would you configure Auto Naming for email aliases?
7. Why might the Permissions tab be missing from the property sheets of directory objects?
8. What is the difference between a *role* and a *right*?
9. How would you give another Windows NT administrator account the permission to administer your Exchange site?

CHAPTER 4

Sites

This chapter looks at the various site-level directory objects that you need to configure when setting up an Exchange site. Topics covered include

- Site-level directory objects
- Site Configuration container
- DS Site Configuration
- Information Store Site Configuration
- MTA Site Configuration
- Site Addressing
- Directory Replication Connector
- Where do we go from here?
- For review

Site-Level Directory Objects

When setting up an Exchange site, there are a number of directory objects at the site level that you must configure. Some of these objects will be present only if additional components are installed (e.g., the Site Encryption Container is only present if Key Manager is installed).

We will look at the most commonly configured site-level objects in this chapter. Because of the vast number of property sheets in Exchange, we can only highlight here those settings which commonly need to be configured. Also, the actual objects displayed in a directory hierarchy depend on which additional Exchange components (e.g., connectors, gateways, Key Manager components, etc.) are installed in your organization.

TIP

Remember, nothing can replace good old hands-on experience with Exchange as preparation for the Microsoft exam!

Shown in Figure 4-1 are the contents of the Configuration container for the site Toronto. The hierarchical structure of a typical Exchange site can be described as follows:

1. The Site container contains two other containers:

   - *Configuration.* This object contains all site configuration objects.

   - *Recipients.* This object contains all recipient objects in the site.

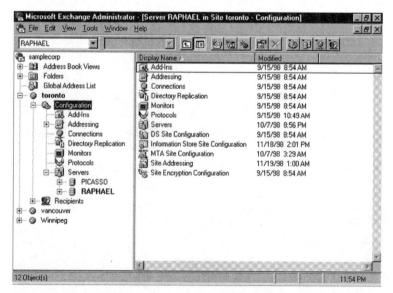

Figure 4-1 The Configuration container and its contents for the site Toronto.

2. The Configuration container, whose contents we are focusing on in this chapter, contains the following objects:

- *Add-ins.* This object contains optional extensions and third-party services.
- *Addressing.* This object contains email address generators used to automatically generate email addresses for recipients and details templates and on-off address templates used for customizing certain Microsoft Outlook dialog boxes associated with addressing, searching, and other functions.
- *Connections.* This object contains connectors for establishing messaging with other sites and mail systems.
- *Directory Replication.* This object contains the Directory Replication Connector that is used to replicate directory information between sites in an Exchange organization.
- *Monitors.* This object contains server and link monitors for monitoring the health of Exchange servers and messaging links.
- *Protocols.* This contains objects for configuring Internet protocols such as HTTP, IMAP4, LDAP, NNTP, and POP3 at the site level.
- *Servers.* This object contains one Server container for each Exchange server in the site.
- *DS Site Configuration.* This object is used to configure certain aspects of the directory service and database for all Exchange servers in your site.
- *Information Store Site Configuration.* This object is used to configure certain aspects of the information store for all Exchange servers in your site.
- *MTA Site Configuration.* This object is used to configure certain aspects of the message transfer agent (MTA) for all Exchange servers in your site.
- *Site Addressing.* This object is used to configure certain addressing and routing properties at the site level.

The objects that we will examine in some detail in the rest of this chapter are

- DS Site Configuration
- Information Store Site Configuration
- MTA Site Configuration
- Site Addressing
- Directory Replication

Other objects will be covered in later chapters in the context of their related topics. But first we will briefly look at the Site Configuration container itself.

Site Configuration Container

The Site Configuration container (called simply the Configuration container in the Exchange Administrator window) is really just a container for holding the various site-level directory objects that you need to configure. The only thing that you can do with this container is use it to change the password for the Exchange *service account* for your site (Fig. 4-2).

Note that if you change the password here, it changes the password for the start-up settings for all Exchange services in your site, but it doesn't change the actual password of the service

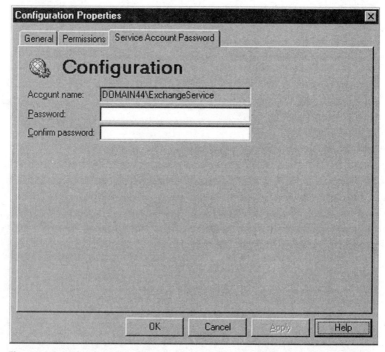

Figure 4-2 Specifying the Service Account password using the Site Configuration object's property sheet.

account itself—you need to also do this using User Manager for Domains. If you don't do this, Exchange services will fail to start.

Now let's go on and look at the main site-level directory objects that need to be configured when you create a new Exchange site.

DS Site Configuration

The DS (*directory services*) Site Configuration object is used to configure certain aspects of the Exchange directory services for all Exchange servers in your site (Fig. 4-3). This is important because the directory database acts as a kind of telephone book for your site's recipients. The directory service is also one of the four core components of each Exchange server and is implemented as a Windows NT service called the *Microsoft Exchange Directory Service.*

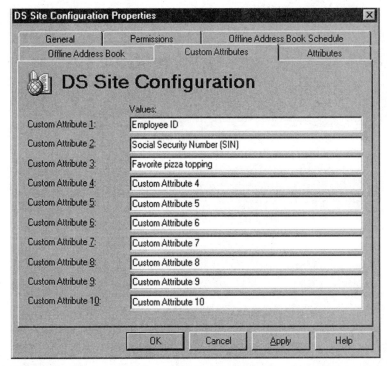

Figure 4-3 Property sheet for the DS Site Configuration object showing the Custom Attributes tab.

Some of the settings you can configure using the property sheet for this object include

- *Tombstone Lifetime.* Remember that the Exchange directory database is replicated among all Exchange servers in an organization. If you delete an object such as the mailbox for user JohnS from the Exchange directory on one server, it still remains in the directory of all other servers in your organization. In order to ensure that the object is purged from the directory of all Exchange servers, the deleted object is replaced with a *tombstone marker,* which is then replicated to all servers in your organization through directory synchronization and directory replication. Each server checks for tombstones in its own directory database according to the scheduled *garbage collection interval,* and if it finds any, they are removed.

- *Anonymous Account.* Sometimes you want untrusted users (users from an untrusted Windows NT domain or from a non-NT network) to be able to have access to the contents of public folders. If so, you need to specify or create a Windows NT account as your anonymous account and then open the property sheet for each public folder and grant some level of *client permissions* on that folder to the anonymous account you specified.

- *Offline Address Book Server and Schedule.* Offline address books are address lists that remote clients can download from your Exchange server so that they can keep a local copy on their computer. This is especially useful for users with laptops so that they can address messages without having to dial in with their modems and then send them later. You can use the DS Site Configuration object to create a new offline address book by specifying which Recipients container it will be based on. If you click the Generate button, the address book will be generated immediately. You should then configure a schedule for the refreshing of all offline address books. The more often you add or delete recipients from your site, the more frequently you should schedule offline address books to be refreshed.

- *Custom Attributes.* Property sheets for mailboxes and other recipients allow you to store personal attributes about the recipients in the Exchange directory database. This includes such things as the recipient's name, address, company, department, home phone number, and so on. But what if this isn't enough? If you would like to store additional information about each recipient, such as their employee ID or SSN number, you can use this property sheet to create custom attributes for all recipients in your site (see Fig. 4-3).

- *Attributes.* You can specify which recipient attributes can be viewed in the address books of authenticated and nonauthenticated clients. In order for a client to access personal attributes of recipients in an Exchange directory database, the client must support the Lightweight Directory Access Protocol (LDAP). Microsoft Outlook and Microsoft Outlook Express are LDAP-enabled clients. For more information on LDAP, see Chapter 11.

TIP

You also can use the Attributes tab of the DS Site Configuration property sheet to specify which attributes of directory objects are replicated to other Exchange sites in your organization. If your sites are connected by relatively slow WAN links, you can reduce replication traffic by only replicating necessary attributes and omitting others.

Information Store Site Configuration

The Information Store Site Configuration object is used to configure certain aspects of the *information store* for all Exchange servers in your site (Fig. 4-4). This is important because the information store acts as a repository for mailboxes and public folders created on your server. The information store is more than just a database; it is also one of the four core components of each Exchange server and is implemented as a Windows NT service called the *Microsoft Exchange Information Store Service.*

Some of the settings you can configure using the property sheet for this object include

- *Message Tracking.* If you enable message tracking for all information stores in your site, the System Attendant service will create a daily log file containing routing information for all messages processed by the information stores. These log files are stored in the directory \exchsrvr\tracking.log and can be analyzed using the *Message Tracking Center,* as described in Chapter 12.

- *Top-Level Folders.* You can specify which users have permission to create top-level public folders (and hence a hierarchy of fold-

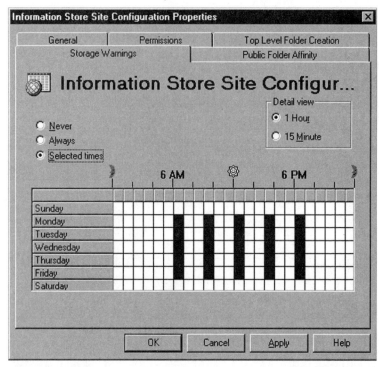

Figure 4-4 Scheduling storage warning notifications using the Information Store Site Configuration property sheet.

ers beneath them). These users also will have the right to assign client permissions to others for accessing the folder hierarchy. You may want to restrict this to department heads.

- *Storage Warnings.* If a user exceeds his or her mailbox quota, a notification message will be sent according to the specified schedule (see Fig. 4-4). Similarly, if a public folder becomes full, a notification will be sent to the folder's contact. This schedule page is similar to many other schedule pages in Exchange property sheets. This one allows you to specify the following times:

  - *Always.* Send notifications every 15 minutes, if conditions warrant it.
  - *Never.* Suspend all notifications.
  - *Selected times.* Drag to select times as desired. Specify either a 1-hour or a 15-minute grid.

- *Public Folder Affinity.* This is explained in Chapter 7.

MTA Site Configuration

The MTA (*message transfer agent*) Site Configuration object is used to configure certain aspects of the Exchange message transfer agent for all Exchange servers in your site (Fig. 4-5). This is important because the MTA on each server is responsible for routing messages to MTAs or information stores on other Exchange servers, to connectors, and to any third-party gateways you have installed. The MTA is one of the four core components of each Exchange server and is implemented as a Windows NT service called the *Microsoft Exchange Message Transfer Agent Service*.

Some of the settings you can configure using the property sheet for this object include

- *Message Tracking.* If you enable message tracking for all MTAs in your site, the System Attendant service will create a daily log file containing routing information for all messages processed

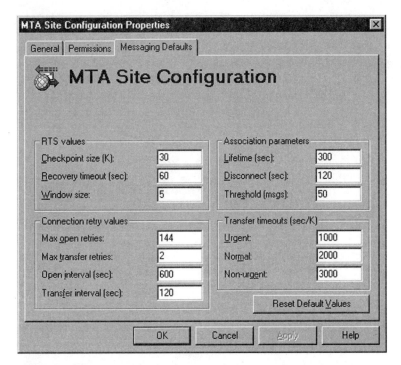

Figure 4-5 Configuring the Messaging Defaults page of the MTA Site Configuration object.

by the MTAs. These log files are stored in the directory `\exch-srvr\tracking.log` and can be analyzed using the *Message Tracking Center*, as described in Chapter 12.

> **NOTE**
> Enabling message tracking for the MTA is different from enabling it for the information store, as discussed in the preceding section. The MTA and information store represent two different core components of an Exchange server, and although both are involved in messaging, they have different functions.

- *RTS Values.* The settings on the Message Defaults page are a variety of options for configuring the MTA (see Fig. 4-5). RTS stands for *Reliable Transfer Service,* and these settings can be modified to ensure reliable messaging takes place. When Exchange is sending messages, it transfers them as a stream of bytes with *checkpoints* inserted at regular intervals. These checkpoints are acknowledged by the receiving server to ensure reliable transmission. If a network error (such as a dropped packet) occurs at some point, instead of restarting the whole message stream, it is restarted from the last checkpoint transmitted. If your network connection is noisy or routers are dropping packets, decrease the *checkpoint size* (kilobytes between checkpoints) to improve speed. This happens because now smaller portions of the data stream are retransmitted when errors occur. If you decrease the checkpoint size on a reliable connection, however, transmission speed will be reduced slightly because more checkpoints need to be inserted into the data stream. *Recovery timeout* is how long the MTA waits before establishing a new network connection and starting the message transfer all over again from the beginning. On unreliable networks, you may want to decrease this parameter, for if the connection times out, the data stream must be restarted from the beginning again. *Window Size* is how many unacknowledged checkpoints can be transmitted before Exchange stops sending data and waits out the recovery timeout. If your network connection is very reliable, you may want to try setting the window size to zero to get the fastest transmission speeds. If you do this, Exchange keeps sending data whether acknowledgments are received or not, and assumes that acknowledgments eventually will come.

- *Association Parameters.* An *association* is a messaging path that has been opened up to another system. Associations are contained within connections, and one connection can contain multiple associations. *Lifetime* specifies how long you want to keep an association open after sending a message—just in case you want to send another message a short time later. *Disconnect* is how long your server waits before disconnecting from a remote system, after it has informed the remote system that it wants to disconnect. *Threshold* is the maximum number of messages that can be queued by the MTA for sending over an association. If this number is exceeded, another association will be opened.

- *Connection Retry Values.* These settings have to do with opening and closing network connections to remote systems for sending messages. *Max open retries* is the number of connection attempts that will be made before a nondelivery report (NDR) is returned to the sender. *Max transfer retries* is the number of attempts that will be made to send a message once a connection has been opened with the remote server. *Open interval* is how long Exchange waits before trying to open a new connection after an error occurs with the existing one. *Transfer interval* is how long Exchange waits before attempting to resend a message over a connection if the previous attempt failed.

- *Transfer timeouts.* These are the timeouts (in seconds per kilobyte) that Exchange waits before sending NDRs, depending on whether the message priority is normal, urgent, or nonurgent.

TIP
Make sure you understand the preceding settings on the Message Defaults page of the MTA Site Configuration property sheet and how they can be used to tune messaging performance.

Site Addressing

The Site Addressing object is used to configure addressing and routing properties for all Exchange servers in your site (Fig. 4-6). This is important because messages need to be delivered successfully from your site to other sites or other mail systems.

Some of the settings you can configure using the property sheet for this object include

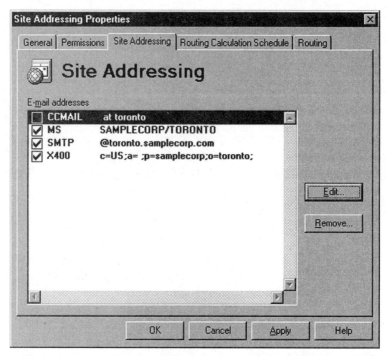

Figure 4-6 Examining the various partial e-mail addresses generated for the site Toronto using the Site Addressing property sheet.

- *Routing Calculation Server and Schedule.* The routing calculation server is the Exchange server in your site that is assigned the job of maintaining the routing table. The *routing table* has information about the various connectors and gateways in your site that act as doorways for delivering messages to locations outside your site. This table needs to be recalculated whenever a connector or gateway is added or removed. This recalculation can take place in three ways:

  - Exchange automatically forces a recalculation when you add or remove a connector (but this may not take place immediately).
  - You can schedule when recalculation takes place using the Routing Calculation Schedule page.
  - You can force an immediate recalculation by selecting the Recalculate Routing button on the Routing page.

For more information on routing and the routing table, see Chapter 15.

■ *Site Addressing.* This tab lists the various partial email addresses that Exchange has generated for your site (see Fig. 4-6). A *partial email address* contains enough address information to locate your site but not any particular recipient in your site. By default, Exchange always generates three different kinds of email addresses for your site (and its recipients):

■ *Microsoft Mail.* The address of your site as far as MS Mail 3.x mail systems are concerned.

■ *Internet Mail.* The address of your site as far as Internet SMTP mail servers are concerned.

■ *X.400.* The address of your site as far as X.400-based mail systems are concerned.

Other types of email addresses (e.g., Lotus cc:Mail) may be generated if the appropriate connectors are installed.

By clearing any of the checkboxes on the Site Addressing page, you can disable the automatic generation of addresses of that type. For example, if you clear the SMTP checkbox, then when you create new mailboxes or custom recipients, they will not automatically have an SMTP address generated for them. Disabling unnecessary address types can reduce network traffic and save disk space when creating mailboxes but also will prevent users from sending mail to mail systems based on that address type. For more information on the various address types, see Chapter 15.

Directory Replication Connector

The Directory Replication Connector object (which is located inside the Directory Replication container—don't get confused by this!) is used to configure directory replication between Exchange sites (Fig. 4-7). This is important because the directory database must be up to date for messaging to work properly throughout your organization. For example, if you create a new recipient object (e.g., a mailbox) in your site and this information is not replicated to other sites, users in other sites will be unaware of the existence of the new recipient and will not be able to send it mail.

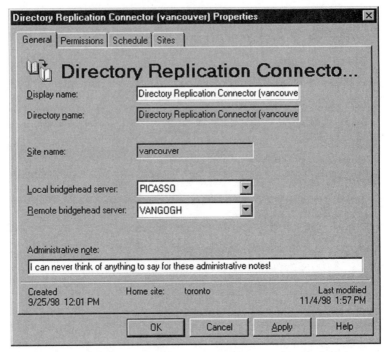

Figure 4-7 Selecting a local and remote bridgehead server for the Directory Replication Connector.

> 📝 **NOTE**
> Remember that directory replication takes place *automatically* between Exchange servers within a site, whereas it must be set up and established between sites.
>
> Also, before you can install a Directory Replication Connector for two sites, you must enable messaging to take place between the sites by installing a *connector* such as the Site Connector for the two sites. See Chapter 10 for more details on connectors.
>
> Finally, note that the preceding four directory objects *always* need to be configured for new sites, but the Directory Replication Connector object *only* needs to be configured if your site is connected to other sites.

Some of the settings you can configure using the property sheet for this object include

- *Bridgehead Servers.* A bridgehead server is an Exchange server that acts as a funnel for messages going from one site to another (see Fig. 4-7). The one in your site is called your *local bridgehead server,* and the one connected to it in the other site is called your *remote bridgehead server.* Of course, from the point of view of an administrator in the other site, these roles are reversed! These bridgehead servers make the actual requests for directory updates from each other, and these directory updates actually pass from one site to the other in the form of email messages. Once updates have been received by a bridgehead server, that server then distributes the updates to all servers in its own site using remote procedure calls (RPCs) in a process called *directory replication.*

- *Directory Replication Schedule.* You can schedule when and how often directory replication takes place between sites. If you frequently create or modify recipients, you should replicate sites frequently, but be aware that if sites are connected by slow WAN links, this may create bottlenecks.

- *Request Now.* This button basically sends a message to the other sites configured to send your site their directory replication updates (called *inbound sites*) saying, "If you have any directory updates, please send them now!" Your own site should be the only *outbound* site listed here, since this is where the Directory Replication Connector sends the updates it receives from other sites.

Where Do We Go from Here?

Now that we have examined the basic site-level properties you need to configure for your new site, we will next look at configuring properties for individual Exchange *servers* in your site.

For Review

Here are a few general questions you can use to quiz yourself. If you are unsure how to answer a question or perform a task, go back and read through the relevant sections in this chapter again.

1. What four directory objects need to be configured for a new Exchange site? What additional object needs to be configured if the site is connected to other sites?

2. What does configuring the DS Site Configuration object do?

3. What are *tombstone markers,* and why are they important?

4. Why might you want to configure an anonymous account?

5. What is an offline address book, and how is such an address book generated?

6. What would you do if you want to store each user's driver's license number in the Exchange directory database?

7. What does configuring the Information Store Site Configuration object do?

8. How do you enable message tracking for information stores in your site?

9. What can a user who has permission to create top-level public folders do?

10. What options do you have for configuring how often warning notifications are sent to users who exceed their mailbox quotas?

11. What does configuring the MTA Site Configuration object do?

12. How does message tracking for the MTA differ from message tracking for the information store?

13. Read the online help for the Messaging Defaults tab of the MTA Site Configuration property sheet, and summarize for yourself the various settings that can be configured.

14. What does configuring the Site Addressing object do?

15. What is the function of the routing table, and why does it need to be recalculated?

16. What is a *partial email address?*

17. What three types of email addresses are automatically generated by Exchange for all recipients and services?

18. Why might you want to disable automatic generation of one or more types of email addresses for your site?

19. What does configuring the Directory Replication Connector do?

20. What must be installed first before installing and configuring a Directory Replication Connector?

21. What underlying mechanism transports directory updates during directory synchronization? During directory replication?

22. What is a *bridgehead server,* and what does it do?

23. How do you force directory replication to occur?

24. What are *inbound sites* and *outbound sites?*

CHAPTER 5

Servers

This chapter looks at the various server-level directory objects that you need to configure when setting up an Exchange server. Topics covered include

- Server-level directory objects
- Servers and Server containers
- Message Transfer Agent
- Directory Service
- Private Information Store
- Public Information Store
- System Attendant
- Where do we go from here?
- For review

Server-Level Directory Objects

When setting up Exchange servers, there are a number of directory objects at the server level that you must configure. Some of these objects will be present only if additional components are installed (e.g., the MTA Transport Stack for RAS is installed only if you plan to install a Dynamic RAS Connector).

We will look here at the most commonly configured server-level objects in this chapter. Again, due to the large number of property sheets in Exchange, we can only highlight here those settings which commonly need to be configured. Also, the actual objects displayed in the directory hierarchy depend on which additional Exchange components are installed.

> **TIP**
> Remember that the best way to become familiar with these objects and their property sheets is hands-on experience, an essential prerequisite for doing well on all Microsoft exams.

Shown in Figure 5-1 are the contents of the Server container for the Exchange server named RAPHAEL. The hierarchical structure of a typical Exchange server can be described as follows:

- The Servers container contains one Server container for each Exchange server in the selected site.

Figure 5-1 The Server container RAPHAEL and its contents.

- The Server container contains the following objects:
  - *Private Information Store.* This object contains all mailboxes homed (stored) on the server. Use this object to configure certain aspects of the *Microsoft Exchange Information Store Service,* a Windows NT service running on Exchange servers.
  - *Protocols.* This object contains objects for configuring various Internet protocols and is covered in Chapter 11.
  - *Public Information Store.* This object contains all public folders homed on the server. Use this object to configure certain aspects of the *Microsoft Exchange Information Store Service,* a Windows NT service running on Exchange servers.
  - *Server Recipients.* This object contains all recipients created on the server, including mailboxes, distribution lists, public folders, custom recipients, and mailbox agents. This is covered in Chapter 6.
  - *Directory Service.* This object is used to configure certain aspects of the *Microsoft Exchange Directory Service,* a Windows NT service running on Exchange servers.
  - *Directory Synchronization.* This object is *not* used to configure directory replication between Exchange servers within the same site, as might be expected. Instead, it has to do with configuring directory synchronization between Exchange and legacy Microsoft Mail 3.x mail systems and is covered in Chapter 14.
  - *Message Transfer Agent.* This object is used to configure certain aspects of the *Microsoft Exchange Message Transfer Agent Service,* a Windows NT service running on Exchange servers.
  - *MTA Transport Stack.* This object is needed only if installing an X.400 or Dynamic RAS Connector on the server and is covered in Chapter 10.
  - *System Attendant.* This object is used to configure certain aspects of the System Attendant, a maintenance service that must be running in order for all other Exchange services to run. Use this object to configure certain aspects of the *Microsoft Exchange System Attendant Service,* a Windows NT service running on Exchange servers.

The objects that we will consider in some detail in the rest of this chapter are

- Message Transfer Agent
- Directory Service

- Private and Private Information Stores
- System Attendant

These four (or five) objects are the *core components* of an Exchange server and are implemented as Windows NT services. Other directory objects will be covered in later chapters in the context of their related topics. First, however, we need to consider the difference between the Servers container and the Server container.

Servers and Server Containers

The Servers container is really just a container for holding the various Exchange servers that are installed in your site. As such, the Servers container is really a site-level object, since it contains all servers in the site. There really isn't much you can do with the property sheet for the Servers container other than change the display name or configure permissions on it (which are then inherited by all the objects it contains). See Chapter 3 for more on permissions.

The Server objects (like RAPHAEL) that are contained within the Servers container are a bit more interesting, however. These are also *container objects* (as opposed to *leaf objects,* such as the Directory Service), and they have a number of configurable properties (Fig. 5-2). Some of the settings you can configure using the property sheet for this object include

- *Location.* Servers within a site can be further grouped into what are called *locations.* This can be useful for controlling access to public folders and is discussed further in Chapter 7.

- *Services.* If you want to use a Server Monitor to monitor Windows NT services on your server, you can specify which services will be monitored here. See Chapter 12 for more on monitors.

- *Locales.* These are different from locations, discussed earlier. Locales have to do with foreign languages and allow currency, date, and time information to be displayed according to each language's conventions. Don't use these unless absolutely necessary because they provide a hit on the server's performance.

- *Database Paths.* This property page displays the locations of your database files (see Fig. 5-2). You also can use this page to move the files to other locations, e.g., if you install an additional hard drive. It is better not to do this manually, but

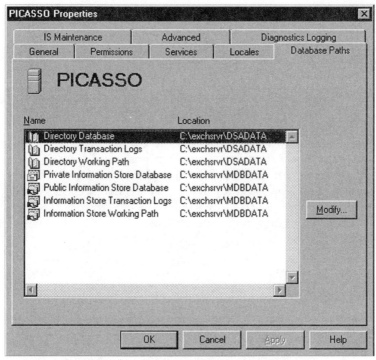

Figure 5-2   The property sheet for the container PICASSO.

instead to run the Performance Optimizer tool from the Start menu and let Exchange decide where to locate the database files. These database files are discussed in Chapter 13.

- *IS Maintenance.* This tab lets you schedule online maintenance for your server's information store (IS), which includes deleting expired messages from mailboxes and public folders and other system tasks. Maintenance should be scheduled when server load is low, since the information store runs more slowly during maintenance periods.

- *Circular Logging.* This is discussed in Chapter 13.

- Consistency Adjuster. This button runs the *DS/IS Consistency Adjuster tool* (see Fig. 5-3). DS stands here for *Directory Service,* and IS stands for *Information Store.* The *raison d'être* for this tool is that certain objects such as mailboxes and public folders are actually located in two different places on an Exchange server. For example, consider a user's mailbox:

- The actual mailbox *contents* (folders and messages) are stored on the user's home server and are located in the private information store on that server alone.

- The *properties* of the mailbox are stored in the directory database, which is replicated to all Exchange servers in the organization.

What happens if an inconsistency occurs between these two locations? For example, what if you restore the private information store from tape backup, and this results in a mailbox existing in the information store but not in the directory database? The DS/IS Consistency Adjuster tool will create the necessary directory object for the mailbox so that it exists in both locations. Some of the settings you can configure for the DS/IS Consistency Adjuster include

- Create a Mailbox directory object if it finds a mailbox in the private information store that doesn't have an associated directory object. Note that if there is a Mailbox directory object without a corresponding mailbox in the information store, it *doesn't* delete the directory object.

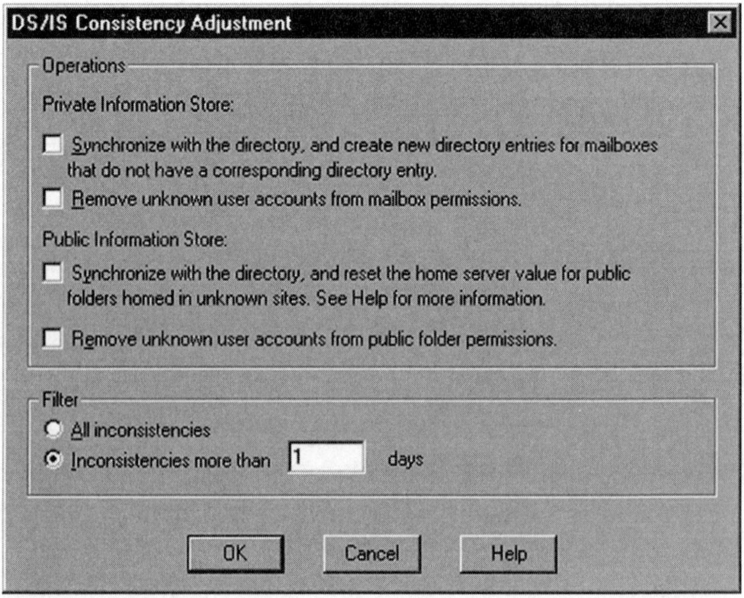

DS/IS Consistency Adjustment

Operations

Private Information Store:

☐ Synchronize with the directory, and create new directory entries for mailboxes that do not have a corresponding directory entry.

☐ Remove unknown user accounts from mailbox permissions.

Public Information Store:

☐ Synchronize with the directory, and reset the home server value for public folders homed in unknown sites. See Help for more information.

☐ Remove unknown user accounts from public folder permissions.

Filter

○ All inconsistencies
◉ Inconsistencies more than [1] days

[OK] [Cancel] [Help]

Figure 5-3 Running the DS/IS Consistency Adjuster tool.

- Create a Public Folder directory object if it finds a public folder in the public information store that doesn't have an associated directory object. Note that if there is a Public Folder directory object without a corresponding public folder in the information store, it *does* delete the directory object. Also, if it finds public folders in the information store that are homed in an unknown site, it homes them on the server on which the DS/IS Consistency Adjuster is being run.
- Remove any users that are no longer valid from either information store or folder permissions.
- You also can reconcile either all inconsistencies or only those greater than a specified number of days (the *latency period*). Use the latter to preserve directory and information store entries when restoring either database. See Chapter 13 for more details.

 NOTE

Do *not* run the DS/IS Consistency Adjuster if

- **You have deleted a directory replication connector to another site, unless you never plan to reconnect the sites again.**
- **You have just joined a site and directory replication has not yet occurred.**

- *Diagnostic Logging.* This lets you configure the logging levels for Exchange server events logged in the Application Log for Event Viewer. You select an Exchange service, specify an event category, and configure a logging level for that category. *None* means that no events are logged for that category, while *maximum* means that practically everything having to do with that category is logged. Avoid too much logging unless you are troubleshooting Exchange services, since excessive logging can slow server performance and eat up mountains of disk space. Diagnostic logging also can be configured for the message transfer agent and the information stores.

Message Transfer Agent

The Message Transfer Agent object is used to configure certain aspects of the *Microsoft Exchange Message Transfer Agent Service,* a

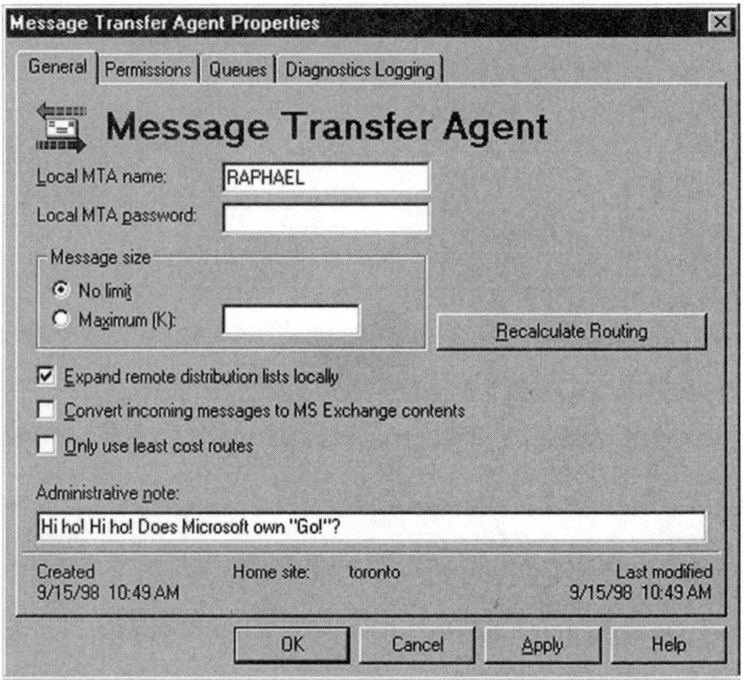

Figure 5-4   The General page of the Message Transfer Agent property sheet.

Windows NT service that is one of the core components of Microsoft Exchange servers. The message transfer agent (MTA) and the information store are together responsible for delivering messages (Fig. 5-4) and perform this task as follows:

- If a message is sent from one recipient to another recipient on the *same* server, the information store on that server delivers the message directly. The MTA is not involved in this transfer.

- If a message is sent from one recipient to another recipient on a *different* server in the *same* site, the MTA on the sender's server gives the message to the MTA on the receiver's server, which then delivers it to the receiving server's information store.

- If a message is sent from one recipient to another recipient in another site or on a foreign mail system, the MTA on the sender's server determines which connector to use to route the message to the remote site or mail system and then gives the message to the selected connector, which then routes the message toward its destination. For more information on routing, see Chapter 15.

Some of the settings you can configure using the property sheet for this object include

- *Local MTA Name and Password.* If you are routing messages to a foreign X.400 mail system, you may need to make the MTA name and password match those of the foreign system (see Fig. 5-4).

- *Message Size Limits.* This lets you specify a maximum message size that the MTA can handle. Anything larger is returned to sender with a nondelivery report (NDR).

- *Recalculate Routing.* This forces the routing table to be recalculated. See the Site Addressing object in Chapter 4 for more details.

- *Only Use Least Cost Routes.* This causes the server's MTA to only attempt to route messages using the least-cost route. If this fails, other possible routes will *not* be attempted, and an NDR will be returned. See Chapter 15 for more on routing.

- *Queues.* Depending on the number of servers in the site and the number of installed connectors and gateways, there may be several different queues holding messages waiting to be delivered by the MTA. If you select a queue here, you can

  - See how many messages are waiting to be delivered in that queue.
  - View the sender's address, message ID, submission time, and size and priority of each message in that queue.
  - Change the priority of a message (but you cannot do this for messages in the Internet Mail Service and MS Mail Connector queues).
  - Delete a message in the queue.

Directory Service

The Directory Service object is used to configure certain aspects of the *Microsoft Exchange Message Directory Service,* a Windows NT service that is one of the core components of Microsoft Exchange servers. The directory service (DS) is responsible for maintaining and replicating information in the Exchange directory database (Fig. 5-5).

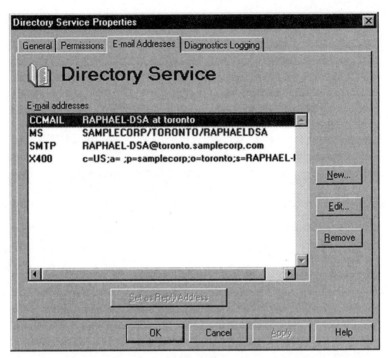

Figure 5-5 Email addresses for the Directory Service Agent (DSA) on server RAPHAEL.

Some of the settings you can configure using the property sheet for this object include

- *Update Now.* All Exchange servers in the same site synchronize their directory databases with each other every 5 minutes, but you can manually force synchronization to occur at any time by clicking the Update Now button. This causes your server to immediately request any outstanding directory updates from other servers in your site.

- *Check Knowledge Consistency.* What happens if your Exchange server is down while a new server or site is installed in your organization? When you bring your server back online, it will have no knowledge of the new server or site. To remedy this, once a day Exchange servers automatically check for knowledge consistency, i.e., that the directory databases on all servers in your organization are consistent with each other. The Check Now button here allows you to force that knowledge consistency check to occur immediately instead of later. If you perform this check and discover a new server or site that your Exchange server was previously unaware of, you should then

- Select Update Now to update your server's directory database.
- Select Recalculate Routing (see Message Transfer Agent above) to rebuild the routing table on your server.

■ *Email Addresses.* This lists the various email addresses for the directory service on your Exchange server. For example, the SMTP address for the directory service agent (DSA) on server RAPHAEL in site Toronto of organization SampleCorp would be

RAPHAEL-DSA@Toronto.SampleCorp.com

NOTE
Since replication between sites usually takes place by means of email messages sent through connectors, it is important for each of the core components of Exchange servers to have its own email address for sending and receiving messages.

Private Information Store

The Private Information Store object is used to configure certain aspects of the *Microsoft Exchange Information Store Service,* a Windows NT service that is one of the core components of Microsoft Exchange servers. The private information store holds all mailboxes for users homed on that server, including the messages and attachments in these mailboxes (Fig. 5-6).

Some of the settings you can configure using the property sheet for this object include

■ *Item Recovery.* Exchange servers can retain messages for a period time even after users delete them from their mailboxes. You can specify either

- A retention time in days, after which the items are permanently deleted.
- Not to permanently delete items until after the information store has been backed up to tape, since they can then be recovered later by restoring the information store from tape.

Using Microsoft Outlook, a user can recover a deleted item by selecting the Deleted Items folder and then choosing Recover Deleted Items from the Tools menu.

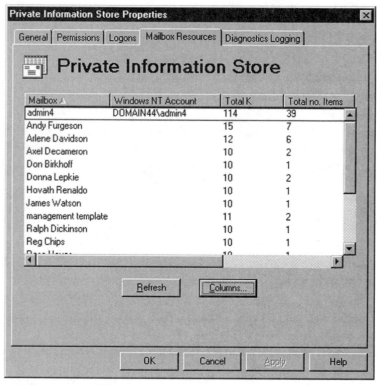

Figure 5-6 Examining the resources used by mailboxes in RAPHAEL's private information store.

- *Storage Limits.* This lets you specify the maximum amount of space the mailbox can occupy in the information store. If this limit is reached, a notification is sent to the mailbox owner. You also can specify separate (larger) limits that, once reached, prohibit the user from sending messages or from sending and receiving messages.

> **NOTE**
> The Prohibit Send option is supported by MAPI clients such as Microsoft Outlook but not by POP3 or IMAP clients such as Microsoft Outlook Express. Also note that these storage limits can be overruled for any particular mailbox by using the Limits page of the property sheet for that mailbox.

- *Public Folder Server.* This lets you specify which Exchange server that users homed on this server will first connect to in order to view and access public folders. If you want to force users homed on your server to create their public folders on a particular server in your site, specify the server here.

- *Logons.* This lets you find out which users and Exchange services are currently logged on to the private information store. Services log on using the *service account* for the site.

- *Mailbox Resources.* This lets you find out how much disk space is being used by mailboxes homed on this server, how many messages are in their mailboxes, and so on (see Fig. 5-6).

Public Information Store

The Public Information Store object is used to configure certain aspects of the *Microsoft Exchange Information Store Service,* a Windows NT service that is one of the core components of Microsoft Exchange servers. The public information store holds all public folder hierarchies and public folder replicas homed on that server, including the postings and documents in these folders (Fig. 5-7).

Some of the settings you can configure using the property sheet for this object include

- *Item Recovery.* Exchange servers can retain postings for a period of time even after users delete them from public folders (see Fig. 5-7). You can specify either
  - A retention time in days, after which the items are permanently deleted.
  - Not to permanently delete items until after the information store has been backed up to tape, since they can then be recovered later by restoring the information store from tape.

  Using Microsoft Outlook, a user can recover a deleted item by selecting the public folder and then choosing Recover Deleted Items from the Tools menu.

- *Storage Limits.* This lets you specify the maximum amount of space the public folder can occupy in the information store. If this limit is reached, a notification is sent to the public folder contact.

- *Age Limits.* This lets you set expiration time limits for public folders, after which postings are deleted.

- *Email Addresses.* See Directory Service above.

Figure 5-7 The General tab of the Public Information Store property sheet.

- *Logons.* This lets you find out which users and Exchange services are currently logged on to the public information store. Services log on using the *service account* for the site.

- *Public Folder Resources.* This lets you find out how much disk space is being used by public folders homed on this server, how many postings and documents are in the folders, and so on.

- *Instances, Replication Schedule, Advanced, Folder Replication Status,* and *Server Replication Status.* These are used to create and manage replicas of public folders on other servers. They are discussed further in Chapter 7.

System Attendant

The System Attendant object is used to configure certain aspects of the *Microsoft Exchange System Attendant Service,* a Windows NT

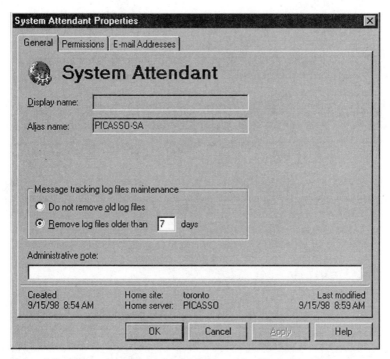

Figure 5-8   The property sheet for the System Attendant object.

service that is one of the core components of Microsoft Exchange servers. The system attendant is a maintenance service that must be running in order for other exchange services to run (Fig. 5-8) and is responsible for such tasks as

- Generating email addresses for new recipients
- Maintaining logs for message tracking
- Monitoring the connection status between Exchange servers

NOTE
If you try to use the Exchange Administrator program to connect to a remote Exchange server on which the system attendant service is not running, you will get the error message: "A connection could not be made to the Microsoft Exchange Server computer *server_name*. The Microsoft Exchange Server computer does not respond."

Some of the settings you can configure using the property sheet for this object include

- *Message Tracking Logs.* This lets you specify whether to keep old log files or discard them when they reach a certain age (in days).
- *Email Addresses.* See Directory Service above.

Where Do We Go from Here?

Now that we have looked at how to configure the main site-level and server-level directory objects, we will next look at creating and configuring *recipients*, which is a large part of the day-to-day task of administering Exchange.

For Review

Here are a few general questions you can use to quiz yourself. If you are unsure how to answer a question or perform a task, go back and read through the relevant sections in this chapter again.

1. What directory objects need to be configured for a new Exchange server? How do these relate to Windows NT services on the server?

2. What is the difference between the Servers container and a Server container?

3. How can you specify which Exchange services should be monitored using Server Monitors?

4. What is a *locale?*

5. Why should you schedule maintenance for the information store during times of low server load?

6. When might you need to run the DS/IS Consistency Adjuster? What does this do?

7. What Exchange services can be logged using diagnostic logging? Where do events relating to these services get logged?

8. How are the information store and the MTA involved in routing messages?

9. When might you need to configure the local MTA name and password?

10. What happens if a message exceeds the size limits of the MTA?

11. How many queues does the MTA have? How can you view messages in these queues, and what can you do with them?

12. How can you manually synchronize the directory database for your server with those of other servers in your site?

13. When might you need to manually run the Knowledge Consistency Checker?

14. What would be the SMTP e-mail address for the System Agent on server RAPHAEL, which is in the site Toronto in the organization SampleCorp?

15. How can you ensure that users have an out if they accidentally delete something important from the Deleted Items folder on their mail client?

16. What kinds of disk space limits can you set for users' mailboxes? What happens if these limits are exceeded?

17. How can you find out how many messages are in a user's mailbox?

18. How can you set expiration time limits for items to be retained in public folders?

19. Why might you want to discard message tracking logs after a certain number of days? Why might you want *not* to do so?

CHAPTER 6

Recipients

This chapter looks at the various recipients and Recipient containers in Exchange and how to create, configure, and delete them. Topics covered include

- Recipients containers
- Creating recipients
- Mailbox
- Distribution List
- Custom Recipient
- Public Folder
- Mailbox Agent
- Where do we go from here?
- For review

Recipients Containers

A *recipient* is someone or something that can receive email messages. The most common example of a recipient is a *mailbox,* which enables a user having a Windows NT account to send and receive messages.

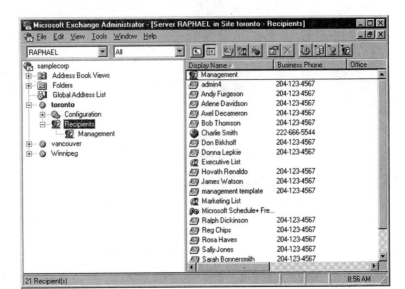

Figure 6-1   The Recipients container for the site Toronto.

Exchange organizes recipients into containers called *Recipients containers*. Each Exchange server has a container called a *Server Recipients container* that contains all the recipients homed (created) on that server. In addition, each Exchange site has a Recipients container that contains all the recipients homed on all the servers in that site.

Figure 6-1 shows the Recipients container for the site Toronto. In the contents pane (right-hand pane) we can see the contents of the Recipients container:

- Mailboxes (admin4, Andy Furgeson, and so on)
- Distribution Lists (Executive List, Marketing List)
- Custom Recipients (Charlie Smith)
- Mailbox Agents (Microsoft Schedule + Free/Busy Connector)

> **NOTE**
> There are no public folders visible in the Recipients container, even though public folders are considered a form of recipient object. This is so because they are considered hidden recipients.

There is also another sub-Recipients container within the site Recipients container. This has the display name Management and contains those recipients which have management functions in the company. You can create as many sub-Recipients containers (and sub-sub- and so on) as you like to organize your company's recipients—the recipients in these containers will still all appear as one long list in the Global Address List. To create a new Recipients container, select the parent container of your choice, and then choose New Other from the File menu.

Hidden Recipients

You can hide recipients from the Global Address Book and from their parent Recipients container. This might be useful at times, for example:

- If you create a template mailbox (preconfigured mailbox for users who will have almost identical mailbox settings), you can create a special container for all your template mailboxes and then hide them so that users won't be tempted to try to send them email.

- If Sally is temporarily on leave of absence from the company, you can hide her mailbox so that she won't be listed in the Global Address List. Of course, people could still send her email directly if they knew her actual email address.

To hide a recipient, you use the Advanced tab on the recipient object's property sheet, as discussed below. To make hidden recipients visible again, use Hidden Recipients from the View menu.

Recipient Templates

We mentioned earlier that you can create a template recipient with preconfigured settings and then use this to create a number of recipients having similar properties. To do this, simply create a recipient (e.g., a mailbox) and give it a name such as Sales Template. Configure all properties that will be common to its derived recipients (in this case, Sales people). This would include such properties as title, address, distribution list memberships, and so on. You would leave blank any settings that are unique to a particular recipient, e.g., name, phone number, and so on.

Now select the recipient template and choose Duplicate from

the File menu. Complete the configuration of the new recipient, specifying the name and other unique properties, and then repeat the process as many times as needed. After you are finished, hide the recipient template from the address book.

Creating Recipients

There are a number of different methods for creating recipients in Exchange, depending on the type and number of recipients being created:

1. Use the Exchange Administrator program to create a new mailbox for an existing Windows NT user. Just choose New Mailbox from the File menu to open a blank property sheet for a new mailbox. Fill in the user's name and other personal properties, configure mailbox settings as desired, and click OK. A dialog box will appear prompting you to either select an existing Windows NT account to associate with the mailbox or create a new Windows NT account based on the autogenerated alias name on the General tab of the mailbox property sheet. To create custom recipients and distribution lists, use the associated commands on the File menu.

2. Use User Manager for Domains to create a mailbox as you create a new Windows NT user. Installing Exchange on a server also installs an extension for User Manager that adds an additional menu item called Exchange (see Fig. 6-2). The new menu options under Exchange include

   - *Options.* This lets you specify the Exchange server on which the new mailboxes will be created and the recipients container on that server and toggles on and off whether to create a mailbox when creating a new account (and whether to delete the mailbox when deleting the account).
   - *Properties.* This opens the property sheet for the mailbox associated with the selected user account.

   To create a mailbox for a new account, just use New User from the File menu to create and configure the properties of the new Windows NT account. When you click Add to complete creating the account, the mailbox property sheet opens up for you to configure the mailbox associated with the account.

3. Use client software such as Microsoft Outlook to create new public folders. This is covered in Chapter 7.

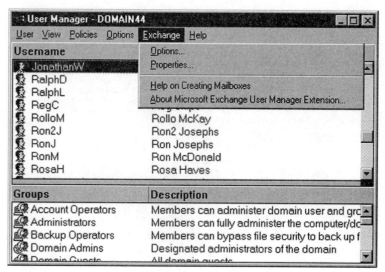

Figure 6-2   User manager for Domains with the Exchange extension installed.

4. Use the Exchange extraction and import tools to migrate existing users from Windows NT or NetWare networks and create mailboxes for them. You also can use these tools for creating mailboxes for a large number of existing users on your network. To do this, first select Extract Windows NT Account List (or Extract NetWare Account List) from the Tools menu of the Exchange Administrator program. Specify the name of a domain controller on the network that has the accounts you want to create mailboxes for, and specify a file for writing the extracted account information to. This file will be a text file with fields delimited by commas (a comma-delimited text file or *.csv file). Edit the file to remove accounts that will not be needing mailboxes. Then use the Directory Import command from the Tools menu to import the *.csv file into your connected Exchange server, creating new accounts along with their mailboxes. This procedure is covered in more detail in Chapter 14.

Mailbox

A Mailbox is a recipient object that enables a user to receive and store messages and their attachments (Fig. 6-3). Mailboxes store their messages and attachments in the private information store

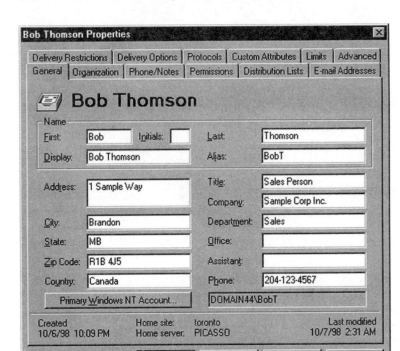

Figure 6-3 Typical property sheet for a mailbox.

on the server where the mailbox was created (the user's *home server*).

Some of the settings you can configure using the property sheet for this object include

- *Personal Information.* This includes name, title, department, company, address, phone, and so on (see Fig. 6-3). The *alias* is the user portion of the user's email address and is usually the same as his or her Windows NT account name. Both the display name and alias name generated for the mailbox can be controlled by using the *auto naming* feature—just select Options from the Tools menu.

- *Primary Windows NT Account.* This is the Windows NT account of the user associated with the mailbox, also known as the *owner* of the mailbox.

- *Organization.* This tab just lets you keep a record of who the user reports to in the organization and who reports to the user.

- *Phone/Notes.* Pretty self-explanatory!

- *Distribution Lists.* This lets you specify which distribution lists the mailbox belongs to.

- *Email Addresses.* This shows the user's autogenerated MS Mail, SMTP, and X.400 email addresses (and other addresses if other connectors such as the Lotus cc:Mail connector are installed). See Chapter 15 for information about addresses.

- *Delivery Restrictions.* This lets you decide who the mailbox will accept or reject messages from.

- *Delivery Options.* This lets the administrator give another user permission to send messages on your behalf. For example, you might give your executive assistant Send On Behalf Of privileges—messages he or she sends will be identified as having originated from the assistant on your behalf. The administrator also can specify here an alternate recipient to receive copies of all your mail, e.g., if you are a temporary worker under someone else's supervision.

- *Protocols.* This lets you specify which Internet protocols the mailbox can use when connecting to Exchange. This is covered in Chapter 11.

- *Custom Attributes.* This lets you specify values for any custom attributes defined using the Custom Attributes page of the DS Site Configuration object's property sheet (see Chap. 4).

- *Limits.* This lets you specify deleted item retention time, disk storage limits, and maximum message size for the mailbox. Deleted item retention time and disk storage limits are defined globally for all mailboxes on the General page of the Private Information Store object's property sheet (see Chap. 5). Settings configured here override the Private Information Store settings. Note that message size limits can be set separately for incoming and outgoing mail.

- *Advanced.* The significant settings here include
  - *Trust Level.* This is used for directory synchronization with Microsoft Mail 3.x mail systems and is discussed in Chapter 10.
  - *Home Server.* If you change the home server here, it will move the mailbox contents (folders, messages, and attachments) to the private information store of the specified server.

- *Hide From Address Book.* Makes the recipient hidden, as discussed previously.
- *ILS Server and Account.* This allows users running Microsoft NetMeeting to connect to an ILS server and request an online meeting with the owner of the mailbox.
- *Outlook Web Access Server.* This is the server running Internet Information Server 3.0 or higher and Active Server Pages (if there is one), which allows users to access their mailboxes using a standard Web browser such as Internet Explorer. This is discussed in Chapter 11.

Moving Mailboxes

Moving mailboxes means moving the contents of the mailbox, i.e., the folders, messages, and attachments that are contained in the private information store on which the mailbox was created (homed). To move mailboxes,

- Use Move Mailbox from the Tools menu to move a mailbox from one server to another server in the *same* site. You also can use the Advanced page of the Mailbox object's property sheet, as discussed earlier.

- Use Directory Export from the Tools menu to move a mailbox from one server to another server in a *different* site. You first export to a *.csv file all the settings for the mailbox or group of mailboxes. Then you use Directory Import from the Tools menu of a server in the new site to import the mailboxes into the private information store of that server. Note that this does not delete the old mailboxes, and you may suggest that the user use Microsoft Outlook's Inbox Assistant tool to configure any mail received by the old mailbox to be automatically forwarded to their new mailbox. After the user has notified all their contacts of his or her new email address, you should then delete the old mailbox.

 NOTE
You also can use Directory Export and Directory Import to move a mailbox from one recipient's container to another. All you need to do is modify the recipients container field in the exported *.csv file before you import it again.

Modifying Mailboxes

If you need to simultaneously modify a property (say, the Department field) in a large number of mailboxes, you can use Directory Export to export the mailbox properties to a *.csv file, modify the fields in question using Notepad or some other text editor, and then import the mailboxes back onto the same server. This will have the effect of batch modifying the fields in question on all the selected mailboxes.

Distribution List

A Distribution List (DL) is a recipient object that enables a message to be sent simultaneously to a group of recipients (Fig. 6-4). The recipients in a distribution list can be mailboxes, custom recipients, and other distribution lists. Distribution lists are used frequently by marketing and sales people for mass mailings.

Figure 6-4 Configuring the properties of a distribution list (DL).

Some of the settings you can configure using the property sheet for this object include

- *Owner.* The owner of the DL is the individual who has the right to modify the membership of the list using client software such as Microsoft Outlook (see Fig. 6-4). The owner also receives error notifications such as nondelivery reports (NDR).

- *Expansion Server.* This is the server that will take a message addressed to the DL and expand it into a series of individual messages for the list's members. If you make heavy use of distribution lists in your organization, you may want to specify a dedicated expansion Server in each site and free that server from other duties.

- *Members.* Click the Modify button to add or remove members using the Global Address List.

- *Distribution Lists.* If this DL is a member of another DL, it shows here.

- *Email Addresses, Delivery Restrictions, and Custom Attributes.* See the Mailbox object earlier in this chapter.

- *Advanced.* Various options set here include
  - Maximum size limit for messages sent to the list.
  - When a user requests a delivery receipt for a message sent to a DL, the delivery receipt can be returned to either or both the user and the list's owner. This also applies to NDRs.
  - You can allow or deny out-of-office messages to be returned by a list's members.
  - You can hide either or both the list and its members from the Global Address List.

Custom Recipient

A Custom Recipient is a recipient that is not part of your Exchange organization (Fig. 6-5). For example, this could be the SMTP address of a user on the Internet, the O/R address of a user in a foreign X.400 mail system, the cc:Mail address of a user on a foreign cc:Mail system, and so on.

When a user in your organization uses his or her client program such as Microsoft Outlook to address a message to a user outside your organization, this can be done in several ways:

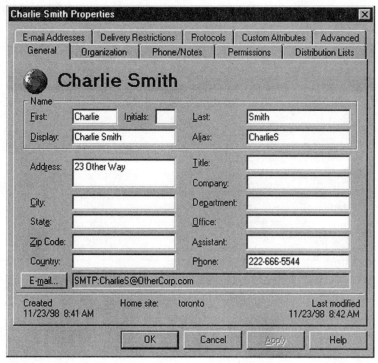

Figure 6-5 A custom recipient and its property sheet.

1. The administrator can create a custom recipient for the foreign user. This custom recipient will appear in the Global Address List, and your users just select it from their Outlook Global Address List and send a message to it. If you expect users in your organization to frequently need to send messages to a specific group of foreign users, creating custom recipients for these foreign users makes life easier for your users.

2. Your users can create *one-off-addresses*, which are one-time addresses for sending a message to a foreign user. In Outlook, they can just type the foreign user's email address into the To field in the new message window or select To, click New, select an address type, and click Put This Entry In This Message Only to open the one-off address template. Fill in the template, and send the message.

3. If you as an administrator don't want the hassle of creating custom recipients, but your users have certain foreign users they frequently send mail to, they may enter these foreign users into their Personal Address Book in Outlook.

 NOTE

- When you create a new custom recipient, you must first select an email address type (e.g., SMTP, MS Mail, X.400, and so on) and specify the foreign user's email address. After doing this, the property sheet for the custom recipient will open, allowing you to further specify what information will be stored on that recipient in the Exchange directory database.

- Also, custom recipients do not take up space in the private information store, since they do not belong to your organization.

Some of the settings you can configure using the property sheet for this object include

- *Personal Information.* This is similar to the Mailbox object above, except that there is normally no Windows NT account associated with a custom recipient (see Fig. 6-5).

- *Email.* This button displays the email address for the custom recipient (which was specified when you created the custom recipient), and it also allows you to modify this address or create a new one.

- Most of the other tabs on this property sheet are the same as for the Mailbox object, except the Advanced tab, which allows you to

  - Send messages to the custom recipient using Rich Text Format (RTF), which includes formatting such as bold, italics, and so on.

  - Lets you specify a Windows NT account that should be associated with the custom recipient, which you normally wouldn't do.

Public Folder

Since public folders are rather different from other recipients, they are dealt with separately in Chapter 7.

Mailbox Agent

A Mailbox Agent is a special recipient object that you don't create. It is actually a .DLL that runs as a Windows NT service and provides some additional functionality to Exchange.

A simple example is the Microsoft Schedule+ Free/Busy Connector (Fig. 6-6), which can maintain information about a user's free and busy times so that meetings can be scheduled using the Calendar function of Microsoft Outlook. This agent is a recipient because Outlook communicates with it by sending and receiving email messages. The property sheets for mailbox agents vary with each kind of mailbox agent.

Where Do We Go from Here?

Having looked at four of the five different types of recipients, we will look in the next chapter at the fifth kind of recipient: *public folders*. We will consider how to create them, configure

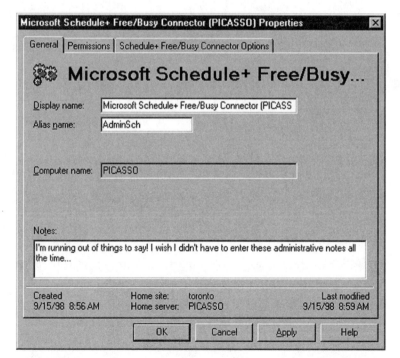

Figure 6-6 An example of a mailbox agent: the Microsoft Schedule+ Free/Busy Connector.

them, and enable easy access to them throughout an Exchange organization.

For Review

1. Name and describe the five different kinds of Exchange recipients.

2. What is the difference between a site's Recipients container and the Server Recipients container for an individual server?

3. How can you create a new Recipients container? Why would you want to do this?

4. What is a *hidden recipient?* Why are recipients sometimes hidden? How do you hide a recipient?

5. What is a *mailbox template?* How can you create a new mailbox based on a template?

6. Why should a mailbox template be hidden?

7. Describe some different ways of creating new recipients in Exchange. Explain when you might use each method.

8. Where is the content for a mailbox stored?

9. What is a mailbox's primary Windows NT account?

10. How can you prevent a mailbox from receiving messages from a distribution list?

11. What are some possible reasons for defining custom attributes for recipients?

12. How can you configure Exchange so that a user can retrieve a message he or she has deleted from the Deleted Items folder in Microsoft Outlook?

13. Explain how you can move a mailbox (a) to a different server in the same site, (b) to a different Recipients container in the same site, and (c) to a different site.

14. What could you do to change the phone number for 500 mailboxes all in one shot?

15. What can the owner of a distribution list do?

16. When might you need a dedicated Expansion Server for your site?

17. How do you modify the membership of a distribution list?

18. Can a distribution list contain other distribution lists? Can it contain itself? What do you think? (Try it.)

19. When might you want to create custom recipients for users in your organization? When might you not want to do so?

20. What is *Rich Text Format?*

21. Give an example of a mailbox agent and what it is used for.

CHAPTER 7

Public Folders

This chapter looks at creating, managing, accessing, and replicating public folders in an Exchange organization. Topics covered include

- Creating public folders
- Public folder properties
- Public folder permissions
- Public folder replicas
- Public folder affinity
- Where do we go from here?
- For review

Creating Public Folders

A *public folder* is a special recipient object that is used for sharing information with other users. Whereas mailboxes are usually owned by a single user, public folders generally are available to all users or at least to groups of them. Users can post messages with attached documents to public folders so that other users can read, modify, or delete them depending on the *client permissions* assigned to the folder.

Whereas a mailbox resides in the private information store of one specific server (the user's *home server*), a public folder may have several *replicas* (copies) that reside in the public information stores of several servers in the organization. Public folder content can be replicated between these servers so that when a user posts a message to one replica, it is soon copied to all replicas of the public folder throughout the organization.

Like mailboxes that exist both in the directory database (where the Mailbox properties are stored) and in the private information store of the user's home server (where the mailbox content is stored), public folders also exist in two places in Exchange:

- The *public folder hierarchy,* consisting of top-level public folders and their subfolders, exists in the directory database of every Exchange server in your organization (if directory replication is occurring properly).

- The *public folder contents,* the messages and attached documents that are posted to public folders, exist in the public information store of the server where the public folder was created (and on other servers if public folder replicas have been created).

Figure 7-1 shows the Exchange Administrator program with the root of the public folder hierarchy selected. The folder Project17 is a *top-level public folder* and has two levels of subfolders beneath it.

 NOTE
Public folders are also contained in each site's Recipients container as *hidden objects.* You can make these objects visible by selecting Hidden Recipients from the View menu. The disadvantage of this view of public folders is that it does not show the hierarchical relationship between the folders but instead lists them all in whatever sort order you have selected using Sort By from the View menu.

One thing that may seem surprising at first is that there is no facility in the Exchange Administrator program for creating public folders. To create a public folder, you have to use a client program such as Microsoft Outlook. Once the folder has been created, it can be configured using the Exchange Administrator program (although certain aspects of it also can be configured using Outlook).

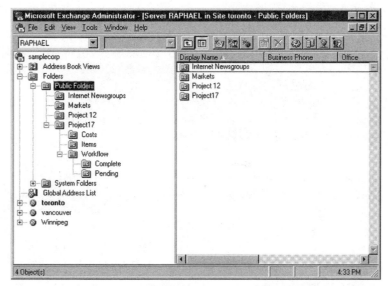

Figure 7-1   The public folder hierarchy for the organization SampleCorp.

Figure 7-2 shows a subfolder being created under the folder Costs, which is visible in the Project17 folder hierarchy presented in Figure 7-1.

Figure 7-2   Right clicking on the Costs folder in Outlook to create a new subfolder.

Public Folder Properties

Unlike mailboxes, several different directory objects are used to configure the properties and behavior of public folders. The rest of this chapter will deal with configuring public folder properties, replication, and affinities.

Once a Public Folder object has been created, its property sheet (Fig. 7-3) can be opened in the usual way. Some of the settings you can configure using the property sheet for this object include

- *Folder Name.*   The name under which the public folder appears in the client's address book can be the same or different from the name of the folder as displayed in the Exchange Administrator directory hierarchy. It is probably best to keep these two names the same to avoid confusion.

- *Alias Name.*   This is the name that is used to address email messages for posting to the folder. For example, using SMTP, a

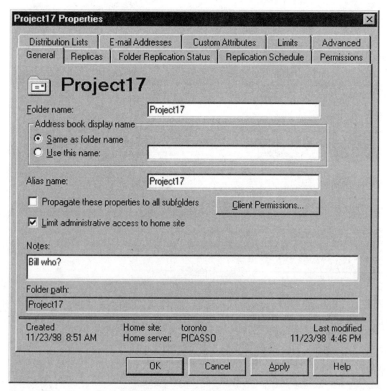

Figure 7-3   Properties of the public folder Project17.

client could post a message to the folder Project17 by sending it to Project17@Toronto.SampleCorp.com.

- *Client Permissions.* These are the various permissions you can set to control access to the public folder. They are discussed later in this chapter.

- You also can propagate the folder's settings to all its subfolders by selecting the checkbox and clicking the Apply button. This opens the dialog box shown in Figure 7-4, prompting you to select which folder properties you want to propagate down the folder hierarchy.

- *Folder Replication Status and Replication Schedule.* These are discussed later in this chapter.

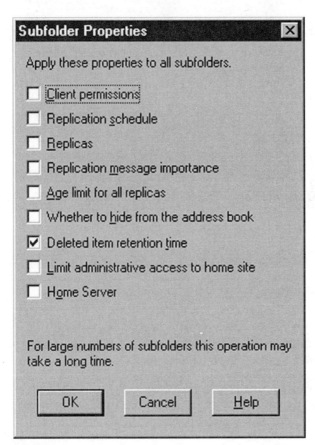

Figure 7-4 Applying selected properties for a folder to all its subfolders.

■ The remaining property pages are similar to those of Mailbox objects and are easily understood (see Chapter 6 for more information on Mailbox properties). The main difference is on the *Advanced* page, where you can

   ▪ See that public folders are hidden by default and unhide them if you choose to.

   ▪ Specify the folder's home server, which is the location of the replica responsible for receiving all messages posted to the public folder. Click the drop-down box to see the location of all replicas of the folder and specify which server will be the folder's home server.

■ *Replication Message Priority.*   The priority you specify here determines the priority of public folder replication messages, which can be

   ▪ *Normal.*   The default priority.

   ▪ *Urgent.*   Specifies that public folder replication messages are to be prioritized as urgent.

   ▪ *Not urgent.*   Public folder replication messages will have a low priority.

Public Folder Permissions

Public folder permissions determine which users are allowed to access public folders and what level of access they will have. Public folder permissions are also called *client permissions,* to distinguish them from *administrative permissions* governing access to the properties of directory objects (see Chap. 3).

To open the client permissions dialog box for a public folder, you can

■ Select the folder in the Exchange Administrator window, open its General Property page, and click the Client Permissions button (Fig. 7-5).

■ Select the folder in the Microsoft Outlook folder list, open its property sheet, and select the Permissions tab.

To grant client permissions to users, click Add to open a list of recipients (mailboxes, distribution lists, and custom recipients), and assign the recipient a *role*. These roles are different from the ones described in Chapter 3 and are summarized in Table 7-1.

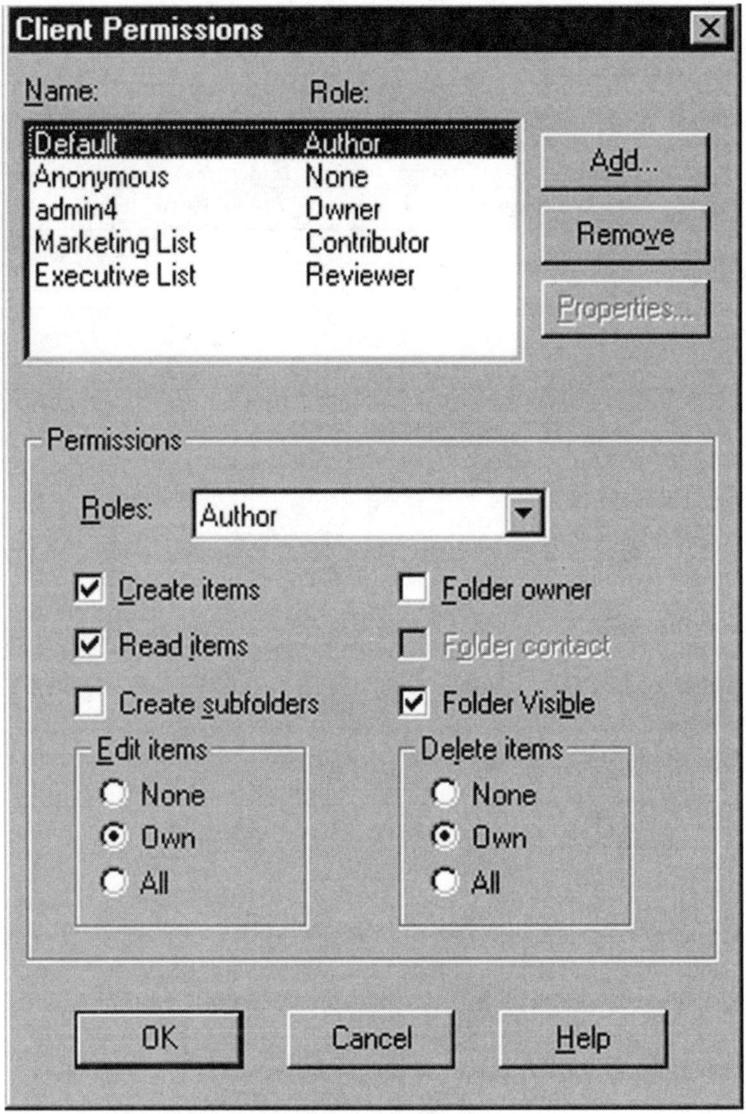

Figure 7-5 The Client Permissions dialog box.

The roles are comprised of different sets of raw client permissions, which are summarized in Table 7-2. You also can define a *custom role* for a recipient by individually specifying the raw client permissions.

Table 7-1   Roles for Client Permissions

| | Client Permissions | | | | | | | |
Role	Create Items	Create Sub-folders	Folder Owner	Folder Contact	Folder Visible	Read Items	Edit Items	Delete Items
Owner	√	√	√	√	√	√	All items	All items
Publishing editor	√	√			√	√	All items	All items
Editor	√				√	√	All items	All items
Publishing author	√	√			√	√	Own items	Own items
Author	√				√	√	Own items	Own Items
Non-editing author	√				√	√		Own Items
Reviewer					√	√		
Contri-butor	√				√			
None					√			

NOTE

When you create a subfolder in a public folder hierarchy, the subfolder inherits the client permissions assigned to the parent folder.

Public Folder Replicas

When users in an organization try to connect to a public folder and read messages posted to it, they may have to cross site bound-

Table 7-2 Individual Client Permissions

Client Permission	Allows users to...
Create items	Create in items in the folder
Create subfolders	Create new subfolders in the folder
Folder owner	Be the folder's owner
Folder contact	Be the recipient contacted when notification messages are generated for the folder by the information store
Folder visible	View the folder in the folder hierarchy
Read items	Read items in the folder
Edit items	Edit items in the folder (either all items or the user's own items)
Delete items	Delete items in the folder (either all items or the user's own items)

aries or even slow WAN links to access the contents of the public folder. For this reason, it is sometimes advantageous to create replicas of public folders. A *replica* is a copy of the contents of a public folder that is stored on a different server's public information store. If a public folder has replicas, then the original public folder is also a replica. In other words, there is no master replica of a public folder.

Replicas are then maintained across multiple sites using public folder replication, which is a similar process to directory replication. Creating replicas for public folders has such advantages as

- Load-balancing access to public folder servers
- Distributing public folder content to other geographic locations
- Providing a hot backup of public folder contents

There are two different ways to create and manage replicas of public folders in Exchange:

1. *Public Information Store object* (see Chap. 5).   Use the Instances, Replication Schedule, Folder Replication Status,

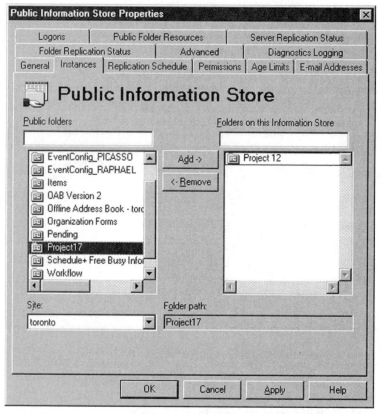

Figure 7-6 Configuring global settings for public folder replication using the Public Information Store property sheet.

Server Replication Status, and Advanced pages. Note that these are *global settings* for the selected server's public information store. Here are the various tabs:

- *Instances.* To create a replica in the selected server's public information store of a public folder on a *different* server, select the site where the folder is located, select the folder in that site, and click Add (Fig. 7-6). The right-hand listbox now shows all public folders that have replicas in the selected server's public information store.
- *Replication Schedule.* This governs the replication of *all* public folder replicas in the selected server's public information store.

- *Folder Replication Status.* This lets you view the replication status of all public folders in the selected server's public information store. You also can view this information by selecting the server's Public Information Store object in the container pane of Exchange Administrator and reading the status information in the columns of the contents pane. Replication status is listed as either

  In Sync. There are no changes to the replica since the last updates were replicated.

  Local Modified. The local replica has been modified and its updates have not yet been replicated throughout the site.

- *Server Replication Status.* This lets you view the replication status (In Sync or Local Modified) of *all servers* in your organization that contain public folder replicas in their public information stores.

- *Advanced.* This lets you specify a smallest time interval for public folder replication and the maximum message size that can be used for replication messages.

2. *Public Folder object.* Use the Replicas, Replication Schedule, and Folder Replication Status property pages. Note that these settings override those set using the Public Information Store object, where applicable. Here are the various tabs:

- *Replicas.* To create a replica of the selected public folder on a *specific* server, select the site where the server is located, select the server from the left-hand listbox, and click Add (Fig. 7-7). The right-hand listbox now shows the location of all replicas of the public folder in the organization.

- *Replication Schedule.* This governs the replication of the selected public folder *only.*

- *Folder Replication Status.* This shows the replication status (In Sync or Local Modified) for all servers that contain replicas of the selected public folder in their public information stores.

TIP
Be sure to understand the differences between using the Public Information Store property sheet to set *global* public folder replication settings and a specific Public Folder property sheet to set replication settings for that folder *alone.*

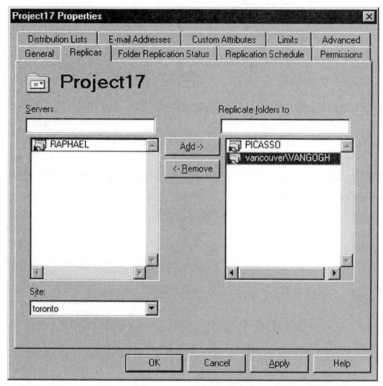

Figure 7-7 Configuring the replication settings for the public folder Project17.

Public Folder Affinity

If users need to access public folders in other sites than their own, but they don't want to replicate these folders to their own site, you can configure public folder affinities. *Public folder affinity* specifies which remote sites a user can connect to in order to access public folders and associates a cost value with each of these remote sites. This *cost value* determines the order in which connections are attempted with the remote sites, with lower-cost sites attempted first.

To configure public folder affinity for your site, use the Information Store Site Configuration object described in Chapter 4. The Public Folder Affinity tab lets you specify a cost value for each site you create an affinity for (Fig. 7-8). Once this is configured,

Figure 7-8   Configuring public folder affinity and its cost values

the right-hand listbox shows all the remote sites that users in your site can potentially use for accessing public folder replicas outside their own site.

When public folder affinity is configured and public folder replicas exist, the general series of events that occurs when a user in the site tries to access a public folder are as follows:

1. If the user's *home server* has a replica of the desired public folder, a connection to the home server's public information store is attempted first.

2. If a connection to the home server cannot be made, or if there is no replica on that particular server, attempts are made to connect to replicas on servers that are in the user's *location*. This takes place one at a time until a connection succeeds or until all attempts fail.

NOTE

A *location* is a subgrouping of servers in a site used primarily to control access to public folder replicas in that site. A user's location is the location specified for that user's home server. The location for a server can be specified using the General tab of the specific Server object's property sheet (see Chap. 5).

3. If no connections to servers in the user's location can be made, or if there are no replicas in the user's location, attempts are made to connect to replicas on other servers that are in the *same site* but in different locations. This takes place one at a time until a connection succeeds or until all attempts fail.

4. If no connections to servers in the user's site can be made, connections with servers in *remote sites* are attempted using public folder affinity and each remote site's cost values. Sites with the lowest cost values are attempted first. Sites without public folder affinity are not attempted at all.

Where Do We Go from Here?

Having looked in Chapters 6 and 7 at the five types of recipient objects, we will next look at how to create *address book views* that can simplify the process of addressing messages for user's client programs.

For Review

1. What is a *public folder?* What can it be used for?

2. Where is a public folder's contents located? Contrast this with the location of contents for a mailbox.

3. What is a *public folder replica?* Why would you want to create replicas of public folders?

4. What is the *public folder hierarchy,* and where is it located?

5. How can you create a public folder?

6. What can you use the alias name of a public folder for?

7. How can you specify which server in your site should be the home server for a public folder? Can this be changed?

8. How are client permissions different from the permissions mentioned in Chapter 3?

9. Describe two ways you can assign client permissions to a public folder.

10. Name the various roles that can be assigned using client permissions, and briefly describe what users having a specific role can do with the selected public folder.

11. What happens to the permissions of subfolders when you configure the client permissions of a parent folder?

12. Compare and contrast managing public folder replication using

   ▪ The Public Information Store object for a server.
   ▪ The property sheet for a selected public folder.

13. What is the difference between In Sync and Local Modified as far as public folder replication status is concerned?

14. What is *public folder affinity?* When would you need to configure it?

15. Which kind of connection to a replica in a remote site is attempted first, one with low cost or one with high cost?

16. What directory object is used to configure public folder affinity for your site?

17. What is the value of grouping servers in a site into subgroupings called *locations?* What directory object do you use to do this?

CHAPTER 8

Address Book Views

T his chapter looks at how to create address book views to provide users with different ways of accessing recipients in the global address list. Topics covered include

- Global address list
- Address book view
- Creating address book views
- Using address book views
- Where do we go from here?
- For review

Global Address List

When users want to send messages using client software such as Microsoft Outlook, they need a way of addressing those messages. They could type in the destination address manually each time, but this would be tedious. They could create their own personal address books, but this is also a lot of work. Exchange overcomes these difficulties by creating a *global address list* (GAL) that contains all recipient objects defined in the organization. Outlook

Figure 8-1 The Global Address List container.

users can then access this list and select recipients for addressing messages.

The Global Address List container contains all mailboxes, distribution lists, custom recipients, and public folders defined in an Exchange organization. The Global Address List container is located directly under the Organization container in the Exchange directory hierarchy, since it is global to all Exchange users (Fig. 8-1).

NOTE
The Global Address List container has no configurable properties.

If your Exchange organization has thousands of recipients in it, the global address list becomes impractical as a tool for users to address messages with, since users will be presented with one long list of recipients in their Outlook address book, which will make for a lot of scrolling. To simplify things for the user, you can create address book views.

Address Book Views

An *address book view* is a grouping of Exchange recipients according to common properties. For example, you could create address book views that group recipients by

- Site
- Home server
- Country
- State
- City
- Department

and so on. You also can create address book views that group recipients by more than one property. For example, you could create an address book view that groups recipients first by country and then by state. In this case, the structure of the address book view might be something hierarchical like this:

```
Country#1
  State#1
  State#2
  . . .
Country#2
  State#1
  State#2
  . . .
. . .
```

Address book views can be created using hierarchical groupings of up to four different properties. These hierarchical groupings are displayed as containers in the Exchange Administrator window, and in the Outlook address book they are also displayed in hierarchical fashion with the associated recipients in each container.

Figure 8-2 shows two address book views created for employees of SampleCorp, our sample Exchange organization.

1. The *By Department* address book view is a simple one-level address book view that organizes recipients into departments. Employees who have the Department attribute configured on their Mailbox object's property sheet are contained within one of the Department containers: Accounting, Management, Sales, or Tech Support. Employees who do not have their Department attribute configured will not be listed anywhere in the By Department address book view.

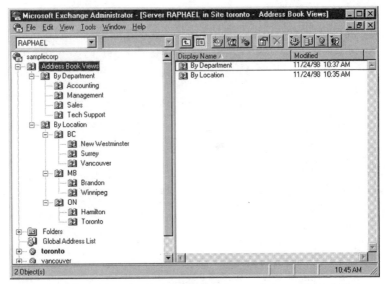

Figure 8-2   Two address book views created for employees of SampleCorp.

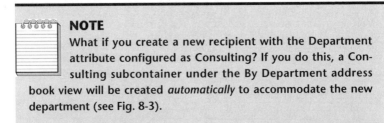

NOTE

What if you create a new recipient with the Department attribute configured as Consulting? If you do this, a Consulting subcontainer under the By Department address book view will be created *automatically* to accommodate the new department (see Fig. 8-3).

---

2. The *By Location* address book view is a two-level address book view that groups recipients first by state (here by province, since we are using a Canadian company as an example) and then by city. Figure 8-3 shows the selected province of BC container with its contents. Notice that its contents include three containers that group recipients by city:

   ■ New Westminster: Sam Smith and Suzy Smith work there.
   ■ Surrey: Sally Stevens works there.
   ■ Vancouver: Ralph Logoine works there, plus a custom recipient Charlie Smith works at another company in Vancouver.

Notice, however, in Figure 8-3 that these five recipients are also visible in the BC container, because since they work at a city in BC, they obviously work in the province of BC as well. This duplication of recipients in address book views of two or more levels of depth can be toggled off, as we shall see later.

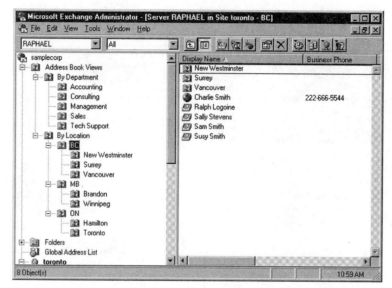

Figure 8-3   An address book view grouped by state (province) and city.

When a user running Microsoft Outlook connects to an Exchange server in SampleCorp, the Outlook address book shows the same hierarchical structure of containers that is seen in the Exchange Administrator window. Compare Figure 8-3 with what Outlook displays in Figure 8-4.

Creating Address Book Views

To create a new address book view, choose New Other from the File menu of the Exchange Administrator window, and select Address Book View. This opens a property sheet for the new address book view, and you are required you to specify at a minimum the following attributes:

- Display name
- Directory name
- At least one Group By attribute (Fig. 8-5).

When you specify these three items and click OK, a dialog box appears stating, "A process has been started to update the Address Book View." Depending on the number of recipients in your organization, this could take some time. After the address book view has been created, it is replicated to other Exchange servers in

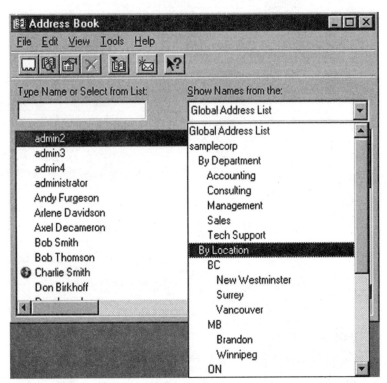

Figure 8-4 How the By Location address book view looks in the Outlook address book.

the organization by directory synchronization and directory replication.

Let's look more closely at the settings you can configure using the property sheet for an Address Book View object:

- *Group By.* You can specify up to four attributes for creating address book views (see Fig. 8-5). This generates a series of nested containers depending on the attributes selected. Attributes you can select include site, home server, personal information, and custom attributes defined using the DS Site Configuration object (see Chap. 4).

- *Advanced.* Using the By Location address book view as an example:

  - If you don't want recipients from Vancouver, New Westminster, and Surrey to be visible also in the BC container, clear the checkbox for Promote Entries To Parent Container.

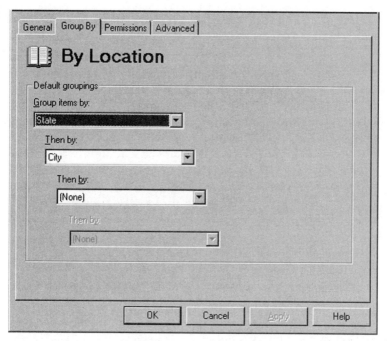

Figure 8-5   The Group By page of the Address Book View property sheet.

- If you want to hide this address book view from the Outlook address book, clear the checkbox for Show This View In The Client Address Book.

NOTE
- The Advanced tab is only visible on the property sheet for the parent Address Book View container, not on the sheets of the automatically generated subcontainers.
- What if you don't have any users yet in Cranbrook, BC, but you want to have an empty container for them anyway in the By Location address book view? Select the BC container and then choose New Other from the File menu, and then select Address Book View Container to create a new Cranbrook subcontainer under the BC container.

- If some of your employees leave Winnipeg so that there are no longer any recipients in the Winnipeg container, note that this container is not automatically deleted. You can delete an empty container manually here. This will improve the appearance of your users' address books.

Using Address Book Views

When an address book view has been created, any user in an organization can use it. This may not be what you intend. For example, let's say that you are providing messaging for two companies using your Exchange server, and you have created a two-level address book called a *By Company address book view* that groups recipients first by company and second by department (Fig. 8-6). The result is that users from either company have access to users from both companies in their client address book instead of being able to see only recipients from their own company. To remedy this situation, do the following:

1. Create two Windows NT global groups, one for company A containing all users in Company A and one for company B containing all users in Company B.

2. Select the Company A subcontainer of the By Company address book view and open its property sheet. Select the Permissions tab, and assign the Company A global group the Search role (Fig. 8-7).

3. Do the same with Company B.

Once you have completed the preceding, each user will have access only to those subcontainers of the By Company address book view for which they have the Search role assigned.

NOTE

If you want to enable anonymous users access to an address book view, assign the Search role to the *anonymous account* specified in the **DS Site Configuration** property sheet (see Chap. 4).

Adding a Recipient

If you change a recipient's properties so that it acquires an attribute that defines it as being part of an address book view, Exchange automatically updates the address book view with this information. For example, if Donna Smith originally had no department attribute specified, and then you modified her property sheet to specify her department as Sales, she will appear in the Sales container of the By Departments address book view.

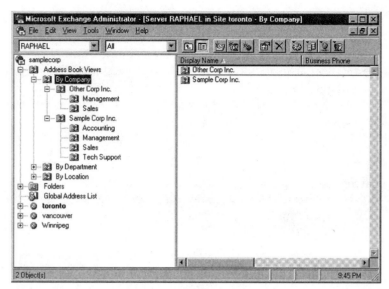

Figure 8-6   The By Company address book view.

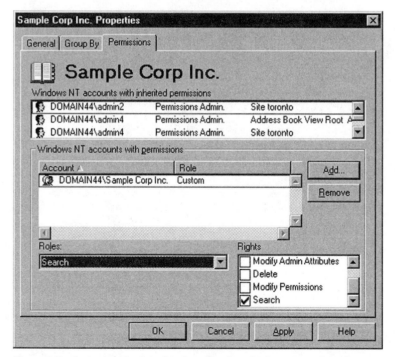

Figure 8-7   Assigning the Search role to the Sample Corp. Inc. global group.

Moving a Recipient

If you move a recipient from one address book view container to another using Add to Address Book View from the Tools menu, the recipient acquires those attributes which define the new container. For example, if Bob Thomson is moved from the Sales to the Tech Support container, his department attribute is updated from Sales to Tech Support.

Where Do We Go from Here?

Having looked at how to set up and configure Exchange sites and servers and create recipients and address book views, we will now look at the various Exchange *clients* and how to configure them to work with Exchange.

For Review

1. What is the *global address list?*

2. What are *address book views?* How do you create them? Why would you want to create them?

3. What attributes can you use to create groupings for address book views?

4. How many levels of groupings can you use to create an address book view?

5. What advanced settings can you configure for an address book view?

6. How can you restrict which users are allowed to access part of an address book view?

7. What does assigning the Search role to a user for an address book view subcontainer allow the user to do?

8. How can you enable an anonymous user to access part of an address book view?

9. How can you move a recipient from one subcontainer of an address book view to another subcontainer?

CHAPTER 9

Clients

This chapter looks at issues concerning client software for Microsoft Exchange implementations. Topics covered include

- Microsoft Exchange clients
- Microsoft Outlook
- Microsoft Schedule+
- Microsoft Outlook Express
- Microsoft Internet Mail and News
- Outlook Web Access
- Where do we go from here?
- For review

Microsoft Exchange Clients

Microsoft Exchange Server provides only the back end of an Exchange-based messaging system—equally important is choosing, installing, and configuring the front end, or client software that users will use for sending and receiving messages. Microsoft

Exchange Server is designed to be compatible with a wide range of Microsoft and third-party client software, including

- *Microsoft Outlook.* This is a full-featured desktop information-management program that provides messaging, scheduling, journaling, and contact-management functionality. Microsoft Outlook is available in 32-bit version for Windows 95/98 and Windows NT, 16-bit version for Windows 3.x, and Macintosh version for Apple Macintosh computers. Microsoft Outlook is included as part of the Microsoft Office 97 suite of applications.

TIP

Although the exam currently focuses on Microsoft Outlook version 8.0 (also known as Outlook 97), you should become familiar with the enhancements in Microsoft Outlook version 8.5 (known as Outlook 98), since Microsoft undoubtedly will upgrading the exam to cover this newer version. Screenshots in this chapter were made using the newer Outlook 98 client.

- *Microsoft Schedule+.* This is the precursor to Microsoft Outlook, and it went through several upgrades until its final release as part of the Microsoft Office 95 suite of applications.
- *Microsoft Outlook Express.* This is a messaging client designed for Internet SMTP mail and NNTP newsgroup access only, and it does not support the desktop information management features of Microsoft Outlook. Microsoft Outlook Express is included as part of the Microsoft Internet Explorer 4.0 suite of client-side Internet applications.
- *Microsoft Internet Mail and News.* This is the precursor to Microsoft Outlook Express, and it was included as part of the Microsoft Internet Explorer 3.0 suite of client-side Internet applications.
- *Microsoft Outlook Web Access.* This is a feature that uses Microsoft Exchange Server combined with Microsoft Internet Information Server version 3.0 or higher to provide client-side access to messaging functions using a standard Web browser such as Microsoft Internet Explorer.

- *Other clients.* Older Microsoft Exchange clients such as the MS-DOS-based Exchange Client and the Windows Messaging client originally included with Windows 95 support limited MAPI-based email functions only and are not covered here. Microsoft Exchange Server also supports Internet SMTP messaging through any RFC-compliant POP3 or IMAP4 mail client such as Eudora, and supports Internet NNTP posting and reading of messages to newsgroups through any RFC-compliant NNTP news client such as FreeAgent. These third-party clients are also not covered here.

NOTE

Of all Exchange clients, only Microsoft Outlook and the older Microsoft Schedule+ support calendaring, journaling, and contact-management functions. All other clients except the original Windows 95 Exchange client are Internet SMTP messaging clients and NNTP newsreaders only.

This chapter is not intended to be a full guide to implementing, configuring, and using Exchange client software. Instead, it will focus on surveying the features of those clients that you need to know.

Microsoft Outlook

Microsoft Outlook is more than just an email client (Fig. 9-1). It is a full-featured desktop information-management program that lets users

- Send and receive email.
- Create and maintain lists of contacts
- Post and read messages to public folders
- Schedule appointments and meetings
- Create and maintain task lists

How It Works

Microsoft Outlook clients use Microsoft's Messaging Application Programming Interface (MAPI) technology to exchange messages

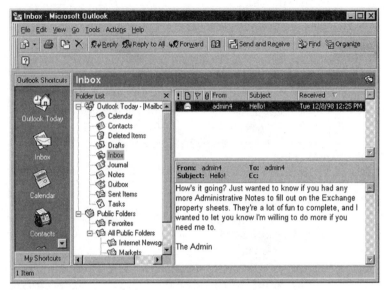

Figure 9-1 Microsoft Outlook 98, the client of choice for Microsoft Exchange implementations.

and other information with Microsoft Exchange Server computers. MAPI provides a uniform set of APIs for messaging functions, allowing developers to easily create client-side software for Exchange that supports messaging and information-management functionality. MAPI essentially acts as a broker between Outlook client-side functions such as reading messages or viewing the address book and Exchange Server functions such as accessing messages in the information store or creating address book views. Outlook uses MAPI calls to send messages through Exchange, read messages in the Exchange information store, access address lists, post messages to public folders, query Exchange for free/busy information of other users to book appointments, and interact with other Exchange Server functions. MAPI enables Exchange Server and Outlook to work together as a truly client/server application. Outlook uses remote procedure calls (RPCs) to access MAPI functions on the Exchange server.

Installation

There are basically two ways to perform installations of Microsoft Outlook: local and shared installations.

Local installations install the Outlook client software directly on the hard drive of the client computer. This option is available for all Outlook versions and platforms and requires only that sufficient disk space be available for the installation. You can perform a local installation by using the Outlook compact disk directly at each workstation (slow) or creating a client installation point on a network server and having each client computer connect to the client installation point to run the setup.exe program (fast). A client installation point is simply a shared folder on a network file server to which users connect using a mapped drive or UNC path in order to run the Setup program. To create a client installation point, share a folder on the file server, insert the Outlook compact disk, run ucsetup.exe, and follow the prompts to supply information as requested.

Shared installations (Outlook 97 only) use less disk space on the client computers by keeping most of the Outlook code in a read-only shared folder on a network file server. Multiple client computers can then connect to this shared folder and run Outlook remotely from their computers. The main disadvantage, of course, is that if the file server becomes unavailable, no one will be able to run Outlook from their computers. To create a shared installation of Microsoft Outlook, share a folder on the file server, insert the Outlook compact disk, run setup /a, and follow the prompts to supply information as requested.

Outlook Profiles

After installation, Microsoft Outlook clients need to have an Outlook Profile (sometimes referred to as a *Windows Messaging Profile*) created for each user who uses the program in order for the Outlook program to function properly. The Outlook Profile essentially specifies three things:

- What messaging service(s) is(are) being used at the back end (e.g., Microsoft Exchange Server, Internet SMTP/POP3 server, MS Mail, and so on).

- Where incoming email is delivered and stored (to Personal Folders or to an information store on an Exchange server).

- How outgoing email is addressed and delivered (using the Global Address List on an Exchange server and/or a personal address book).

> ### NOTE
> The Outlook Profile of a user is not the same as the user's Windows 95/98 or Windows NT User Profile. The Outlook Profile is contained within a user's User Profile. If all User Profiles are stored on a network file server in order to provide users with roaming profiles, then users also will be able to access their messages from any computer on the network using Microsoft Outlook.

Outlook Profiles can be created manually on computers where Microsoft Outlook has been installed by using the Mail utility (sometime called the Mail and Fax utility) in Control Panel or by using Services from the Tools menu in Microsoft Outlook. To see the available services you can configure, start the Mail utility and click Add to open the Add Service to Profile dialog box (Fig. 9-2).

The explanation of these installable information services is as follows:

- *Exchange Server.* Used to configure a Microsoft Exchange Server as the back end to a Microsoft Outlook-based messaging system.

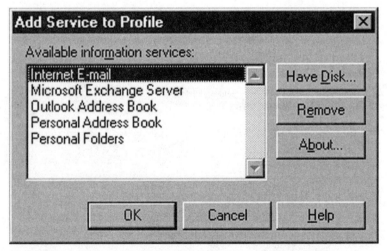

Figure 9-2 Adding a new information service to an Outlook Profile.

- *Internet Mail.* Used to configure an Internet SMTP host as the back end of a Microsoft Outlook-based messaging system.

- *Microsoft Mail.* Used to configure a Microsoft Mail 3.x postoffice as the back end of a Microsoft Outlook-based messaging system.

- *Outlook Address Book.* Supports the functions of the Outlook Contacts folder by storing email addresses of all entries in the Contacts folder.

- *Personal Address Book.* A file with the extension *.pab that usually is located on the client computer and allows users to maintain their own personal address lists or copy them from other lists such as the Global Address List on an Exchange server.

- *Personal Folders.* A file with the extension *.pst that usually is located on the client computer and acts as a delivery point for incoming messages to be delivered.

NOTE

The Personal Address Book (*.pab) and Personal Folders (*.pst) files can be stored either on the client computer or on a network share. Placing them on a network share enables users to access them from anywhere on the network (roaming users). However, if Exchange Server is your messaging system back end, you should configure the Exchange Server information service to store users' messages in the servers' Information Store instead of enabling Personal Folders for your users. One reason for this is that *.pst files have a maximum size of 2 GB. Another is that they are password protected by a password the user specifies, and if the user forgets his or her password, there is no way to reset it—the messages are gone forever.

One possible use for *.pst files is if you are in the process of migrating a Microsoft Mail 3.x messaging system to Exchange. During the migration process, users may have both MS Mail mailboxes and Exchange mailboxes. To simplify access to their mail, they can configure Outlook to download messages from both mail systems to a single location, a *.pst file either on the user's client machine or on a network file server. This way users can receive all their mail to a single location instead of having to check for mail twice. This will work even if there is no messaging connectivity between the two mail systems during the migration process.

There are several files that can be used by administrators to simplify the creation and configuration of Outlook Profiles for their users:

- `Outlook.prf`. This file can be found on the Microsoft Office 97 and Microsoft Outlook compact disks. Administrators can customize this file before installing Outlook on client machines and use it in conjunction with the `Newprof.exe` utility to automatically generate Outlook Profiles for each user when they install or first start Microsoft Outlook. Note that a unique `Outlook.prf` file is needed for every unique Outlook Profile to be created, each containing information such as the user's mailbox name and home server.

- `Exchange.prf`. This file can be found on the Microsoft Office 97 Resource Kit compact disk and should be used in place of `Outlook.prf` if your deployment of Microsoft Outlook is to use Microsoft Exchange Server as its messaging service. The reason is that the `Outlook.prf` file generates Outlook Profiles that specify each user's local Personal Folders (`*.pst`) file as their default message store, rather than using the Information Store on the Exchange server to store their messages. To use the `Exchange.prf` file, copy it to your client installation point, delete the `Outlook.prf` file, and rename `Exchange.prf` to `Outlook.prf`. Then open it using Notepad and find the line:

  ```
  HomeServer =
  ```

  and add the name of the Exchange server on which the user's mailbox is homed.

- `None.prf`. An alternative for administrators is to replace the `Outlook.prf` file with a different file from the Microsoft Outlook compact disk, namely, `None.prf`. When users first start Outlook on their computers, this will cause the Outlook Setup Wizard to start. Provide users with written instructions on how to complete the Wizard.

- `Profgen.exe`. An alternative to using the preceding files is to use the Microsoft Exchange Roving User Profile Generator Program (`Profgen.exe`). This is an unsupported program that creates a new Outlook Profile using users' Windows NT account information and does not require creating custom `Outlook.prf` files for each user. In order for `Profgen.exe` to work, a user's Windows NT user name and his or her Exchange Server alias name must be the same.

Other Outlook Options

Space doesn't permit complete coverage of all Microsoft Outlook configuration options, but there are a few that are worth zeroing in on.

OFFLINE FOLDERS

If you want to use Outlook to work with the contents of an Exchange Server-based folder while off-line (disconnected from the Exchange server), you can use Offline Folders. Your Offline Folders are stored in a file formatted similarly to a *.pst file, except that it is called an Offline Store or *.ost file. To make a server-based folder available for off-line use, open the property sheet of the folder in Outlook, select the Synchronization tab, and specify that the folder should be made available for off-line use. This will copy the contents of the server-based folder to the local *.ost file on your hard drive.

Offline Folders are a good way to enable users to access their mailboxes both locally when at work and remotely when traveling with laptop computers. When using Offline Folders, note that

- Making any of the following folders available for off-line use makes all of them available for off-line use:
  Inbox
  Outbox
  Deleted items
  Sent items
  Contacts
  Tasks
  Journal
  Notes

- To make public folders available for off-line use, they must first be identified as Favorites. You can do this by first copying these public folders to your Favorites folder in Microsoft Outlook and then specifying that the folder be available for both off-line and on-line use by accessing the Synchronization tab of the folder's property sheet.

- When you modify the contents of folders identified for off-line use, you need to synchronize these changes back to the server-based copies of those folders. Use the Synchronize option from the Tools menu to either

- *Manually* synchronize Offline Folders with their server-based copies.
- Configure Offline Folders to be *automatically* synchronized each time the user exits Outlook.

- While the *.pst file can be copied to another computer and used, the *.ost file cannot.

REMOTE MAIL

When a Microsoft Outlook client is configured to use Remote Mail, a user can establish a connection to an Exchange Server, view a list of messages waiting to be retrieved from the server, and select which of these messages the user wants to download to the client machine. Remote Mail typically is used when users dial in remotely using laptops. This allows users to select which messages to download and which to leave unread on the server—typically messages with large attachments or dealing with unimportant issues can be left unread on the server.

To configure Remote Mail on an Outlook client, open the Outlook Profile using the Services option on the Tools menu, open the properties of the Microsoft Exchange Server information service, and then configure the settings on the Dial-Up Networking and Remote Mail tabs (Fig. 9-3). Specifically, the Dial-Up Networking tab allows you to specify a Dial-Up Networking (DUN) connection to be used for Remote Mail access. The Remote Mail tab lets you specify whether to

- Download only mail items that you mark for retrieval
- Filter items for retrieval by From or Subject fields and whether the messages are directly addressed to the user or copied (cc'd). In addition, using the Advanced button, you can filter messages by size in kilobytes, date received, importance, sensitivity, whether the messages contain attachments, whether the messages are unread, or messages that do *not* meet the selected criteria (logical NOT).
- Schedule when and how often Remote Mail should connect to download mail.

To start using Remote Mail, use Remote Mail from the Tools menu.

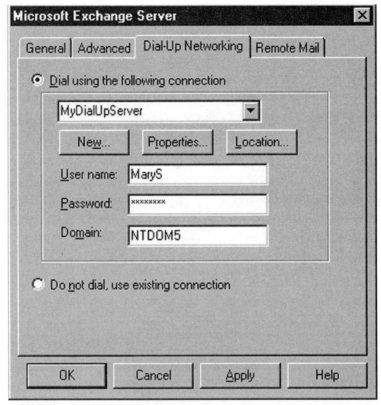

Figure 9-3 Configuring the Dial-Up Networking tab of the Microsoft Exchange Server information services property sheet.

TIP
Remember, Microsoft Exams test your hands-on experience with a product. You should spend time experimenting with Offline Folders, Remote Mail, and other features of Microsoft Outlook. Nothing prepares you better for an exam than hands-on experience with the product.

DELEGATE ACCESS

Sometimes you may want another user to create and send messages on your behalf, for example, when you are going on a trip and want your assistant to send messages on your behalf. Microsoft Outlook allows you to configure several kinds of delegate access:

- *Send On Behalf Of.* This places your delegate's name in the From field of the message while indicating your own name as Sent On Behalf Of.

- *Send As.* This is a little stronger—the message actually appears to be From you, and your delegate's name does not appear anywhere in the message.

To configure Send On Behalf Of delegate access, you need to do two things:

1. Use the Options selection from the Tools menu, select the Delegates tab, and click Add to select your delegate from the Global Address List.

2. In the Delegate Permissions dialog box that appears next, specify which folders you want to make available to your delegate and what kind of access to those folders you want to grant to your delegate (Fig. 9-4).

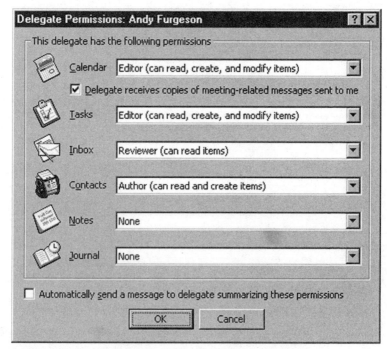

Figure 9-4 Granting your delegate access to your mail folders.

NOTE
The Exchange Administrator program also can configure
Send On Behalf Of delegate access for a user by using the
Delivery Options tab of the user's Mailbox property sheet.

To configure Send As delegate access, you need to do the
following:

1. Access the property sheet of the Mailbox folder in Microsoft
   Outlook, and select the Permissions tab.

2. Click Add to select your delegate from the Global Address List,
   and then specify the level of permissions you want to grant to
   your delegate.

Finally, for both kinds of delegate access, the delegate needs to
add your own mailbox to his or her Microsoft Exchange Server
information service properties, which will allow him or her to see
and access your mailbox, according to the permissions you have
granted him or her.

ASSISTANTS

Microsoft Outlook includes two assistants:

- *Inbox Assistant.* Use this to generally configure how incoming
  mail is handled. Note that in the more recent version, Outlook
  98, this feature is replaced by the Rules Wizard.

- *Out of Office Assistant.* Use this to specifically configure how
  incoming mail is handled when you are out of the office, for
  example, on vacation.

These Assistants handle incoming mail by using a series of *rules*
you create. These rules examine aspects of incoming messages
and process the messages accordingly. For example, you could
create a rule that forwards a copy of all incoming mail to an SMTP
host at your Internet service provider (ISP) so that you can access
your work mail at home by dialing into your ISP.

FORMS AND FORM LIBRARIES

Forms are graphic interfaces presented to users for creating, viewing, or modifying messages. Forms typically are created as user

interfaces to public folders and allow information stored in these folders to be entered and displayed in a standardized format. Forms are used to build collaborative applications for multiple users to work together on a project. Examples of collaborative applications using forms include such things as

- Bulletin boards
- Purchase orders
- Help desk request forms

Microsoft Outlook includes an optional component called the *Outlook Forms Designer* for creating and configuring Outlook forms. Forms created by the Outlook Forms Designer can be saved as *.oft files and published to public folders. Outlook Forms can be designed by selecting Forms from the Tools menu.

Forms are stored in *forms libraries* on Exchange servers. There are several types of forms libraries:

- *Organization Forms Library.* This contains forms that are accessible to anyone in the Exchange organization and is located in a system public folder on an Exchange server. The forms should be replicated to all other sites in your organization. An organization forms library can be created using Forms Administrator from the Tools menu of the Exchange Administrator program. Usually only administrators have the permission to install new forms in the Organization Forms Library. The Organization Forms Library is only accessible to users who are on-line.

- *Personal Forms Library.* This consists of forms that are only accessible to you as an Exchange user and are stored in your mailbox, that is, in the private information store of your home server. When Microsoft Outlook is installed and configured on a client machine, a Personal Forms Library is created for the user of that machine. A user's Personal Forms Library is accessible whether the user is on-line or off-line.

- *Folder Forms Library.* This consists of forms that are installed on a particular public folder and are available to all users who have been granted access to that public folder.

Microsoft Schedule+

Microsoft Schedule+ is an older Microsoft Exchange client designed originally for Microsoft Mail 3.x messaging systems that provides similar but not as sophisticated scheduling capabilities as Microsoft Outlook does. The only things you need to know about Microsoft Schedule+ are

- Both Microsoft Outlook and Microsoft Schedule+ make use of the Schedule+ Free/Busy Connector on Microsoft Exchange to exchange free/busy information between users for making appointments. This connector is a type of Mailbox Agent and is found in the site Recipient's container.

- In addition, both Microsoft Outlook and Microsoft Schedule+ make use of the Schedule+ Free/Busy Information system public folder, which needs to be replicated between all sites in an Exchange organization to allow users to make appointments and book meetings with other users in the organization.

- Microsoft Outlook users can schedule meetings and send messages to Microsoft Schedule+ users, and vice versa. Both client programs also can be used in a mixed Microsoft Exchange and Microsoft Mail network. These platforms are interoperable to a certain extent, but full functionality is best achieved by upgrading Schedule+ to Outlook and migrating MS Mail systems to Exchange. If Outlook and Schedule+ are both installed on users' computers, they can import their Schedule+ calendars into Outlook using Import and Export from the File menu in Outlook.

Microsoft Outlook Express

Microsoft Outlook Express is a popular Internet mail and news client included with Microsoft Internet Explorer 4.0. Microsoft Outlook Express supports Internet access only to Exchange servers, using the standard Internet protocols:

- SMTP for sending Internet mail
- POP3 and IMAP4 for downloading Internet mail
- NNTP for accessing USENET newsgroups
- LDAP for accessing personal information about users stored in the Microsoft Exchange directory database
- S/MIME for sending secure email using digital signatures and public-key encryption
- HTML for sending and receiving rich text messages in HTML format

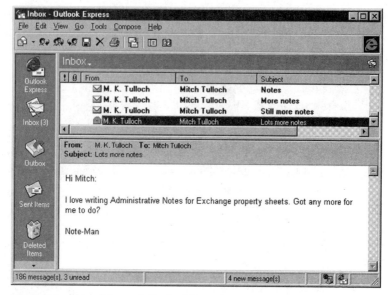

Figure 9-5 Using Microsoft Outlook Express.

To use Microsoft Outlook Express in your Exchange organization, you must have the Internet Mail Service installed on at least one Exchange server (Fig. 9-5). Internet access to Exchange is covered in detail in Chapter 11.

Microsoft Internet Mail and News

Microsoft Internet Mail and News is an older Internet mail client included with Microsoft Internet Explorer 3.0. It has less functionality that Outlook Express and doesn't support IMAP4, LDAP, or S/MIME protocols.

Outlook Web Access

Outlook Web Access is an Exchange technology that allows users to use a standard Internet Web browser such as Microsoft Internet Explorer to

- Securely access their email on Microsoft Exchange servers
- Access the personal scheduling and collaboration functions of Microsoft Outlook that are supported by Exchange Server

- Access public folders and the Global Address List
- Do these things using a standard Web browser running on any operating system platform

Before you install Outlook Web Access on an Exchange computer, you must have Microsoft Internet Information Server version 3.0 or higher installed on a computer in your network. This computer also should have Active Server Pages (ASP) technology installed on it.

To use a Web browser to access your Exchange system (Fig. 9-6):

1. Open the following URL in your browser:

   ```
   http://IIS_server_name/exchange
   ```

2. In the opening screen of Outlook Web Access, enter your mailbox alias name and press ENTER.

3. In the next screen, enter your logon credentials in the form:

   ```
   domain_name\user_name
   password
   ```

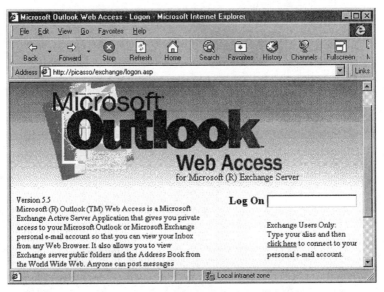

Figure 9-6   Accessing an Exchange server from a Web browser using Outlook Web Access.

Now you can access your mail, calendar, and public folders using your Web browser.

Where Do We Go from Here?

Having looked at various Exchange clients and how to configure them, we will next look at the various *connectors* that can be used to establish messaging connectivity between Exchange sites and with foreign mail systems.

For Review

1. Name and describe the various clients available for Microsoft Exchange, and describe when you might use each of them.

2. What is the underlying mechanism by which Microsoft Outlook interacts with Exchange servers?

3. Describe the two different ways of installing Microsoft Outlook.

4. What is an *Outlook Profile?* How do you create it? What information services can it contain?

5. Describe the purpose and use for each of the following:
   - A *.pst file
   - A *.pab file
   - An *.ost file

6. What are the different *.prf files, and what are they used for?

7. What does the utility Newprof.exe do?

8. What does the utility Profgen.exe do?

9. What are *Offline Folders,* and when would they be useful to implement?

10. Describe two ways of synchronizing Offline Folders.

11. What can users do if Remote Mail is configured on their Outlook clients?

12. What filtering options are available using Remote Mail?

13. What two types of Delegate Access can be configured for users, and how can you configure them?

14. What are *rules?* Where are they used?

15. What are *forms?* How can they be used?

16. Compare and contrast the Organizational Forms Library with a Personal Forms Library.

17. What components of Microsoft Exchange Server enable users of Microsoft Outlook or Microsoft Schedule+ to make appointments with each other?

18. What Internet protocols does Microsoft Outlook Express support?

19. When would you install Outlook Express on client machines?

20. What is *Internet Mail and News?*

21. What must be done to enable users to access their mail using a standard Web browser such as Microsoft Internet Explorer?

CHAPTER 10

Connectors

This chapter looks at how to establish messaging connectivity between different sites in an Exchange organization and between an Exchange organization and a foreign mail system. The chapter also examines the different email address types used by Exchange and how these are used to route messages between servers, sites, and mail systems. Topics covered include

- Overview of connectors
- Addressing
- Routing
- Connections Container
- Site Connector
- Dynamic RAS Connector
- X.400 Connector
- MS Mail Connector and dirsync
- Connector for cc:Mail
- Where do we go from here?
- For review

Overview of Connectors

Connectors are components of Microsoft Exchange Server that can be used to establish messaging connectivity between one Exchange site and another in the same organization or between one Exchange organization and a foreign mail system. Foreign mail systems can refer to

- A different Microsoft Exchange organization
- A Microsoft Mail 3.x network
- A Lotus cc:Mail messaging system
- An X.400-based messaging system, which is common in Europe
- A mainframe-based messaging system such as PROFS and SNADS
- The SMTP-based mail system of the Internet or a private SMTP network

When a connector is installed on an Exchange server, the connector acts as a kind of funnel or gateway for routing messages of a particular type to another site or mail system. Connectors are distinguished both by the type of network connectivity they establish (permanent or dial-up) and by the type of email addresses they can handle (SMTP, X.400, MS Mail, and so on). Table 10-1 shows the different types of connectors and what they are used for.

 NOTE
The Internet Mail Service and other aspects of Internet connectivity with Exchange are covered in Chapter 11.

Addressing

Microsoft Exchange sends email messages using addresses. These addresses can be of various types. When a typical installation of Exchange is performed, three types of email addresses are automatically created for every directory object that can receive a message. This means that every Exchange service and recipient in an

Table 10-1   Different Types of Connectors and What They Can Be
Used For

| | Can Be Used to Connect to... | |
| | Another | A Foreign |
Connector	Site	Mail System
Site connector	√	
Dynamic RAS connector	√	
X.400 connector	√	√
Internet mail service	√	√
Connector for cc: Mail		√
MS mail connector		√

organization has three email addresses. These three types of
addresses are

1. X.400
2. Internet (SMTP)
3. MS Mail (for PC networks)

In addition, a *distinguished name* (DN) is automatically created
for every object in the Exchange directory. This is also a kind of
address, but it is used internally by Exchange—you cannot use
the distinguished name of a mailbox to address mail to that
mailbox.

If custom components such as the Lotus cc:Mail connector
were installed during setup, directory objects also will have a
cc:Mail address automatically generated. Every time you create a
new Exchange recipient (mailbox, distribution list, custom recipient, or public folder), a DN will be created automatically for the
recipient, along with X.400, SMTP, and MS Mail addresses, plus
addresses for any custom connector types installed.

Let's now look at each of these different types of addresses,
starting with the internally used distinguished name (DN).

Distinguished Name

Every object in the Exchange directory database is identified by a distinguished name, or DN. This is true whether or not that directory object is capable of receiving email messages or not. Distinguished names are part of the X.500 directory recommendation proposed by the International Telecommunications Union (ITU), the specification after which the Exchange directory was modeled. Distinguished names consist of a hierarchical set of attributes that uniquely identifies the directory object. The DN is in effect a kind of path to locate an object in the Exchange directory.

As an example, consider a user Mary Smith whose mailbox MaryS is located in the site Toronto of the organization SampleCorp. The DN for Mary Smith's mailbox would be

```
o = SampleCorp/ou = Toronto/cn = recipients/cn = MaryS
```

This DN says that mailbox MaryS is located in the Recipients container of site Toronto in organization SampleCorp. The DN consists of four attributes composed of three basic types:

- o for organization name
- ou for site name
- cn for common name, which is used for every directory object that is not a site or an organization

X.400

X.400 is an ITU standard for a global messaging system that is used widely in Europe. X.400 addresses are also known as *Originator/Recipient addresses,* or simply *O/R addresses,* and also consist of a hierarchical set of attributes that uniquely identifies an object within a global messaging system. O/R addresses are generated automatically by Exchange for all directory objects that can receive email messages. This includes recipients and Exchange services such as the Directory Replication service.

Here is what the X.400 address for the mailbox of Mary Smith would look like, following the previous example:

```
c = ca;a =   ;p = samplecorp;o = toronto;s = smith;g = mary;
```

Here is what each of the preceding O/R attributes represent:

- c is the country name, here Canada.

- a is the Administrative Management Domain (ADMD). This would be the telecommunications company for a foreign X.400 mail system and could be Sprint, MCI, and so on. It is left blank in the example to illustrate that we are using X.400 messaging internally in the Exchange organization.

- p stands for Private Management Domain (PRMD), which is the name of our Exchange organization SampleCorp.

- o stands for organization, which in this case refers not to the Exchange organization but to the Exchange site name Toronto.

- s stands for surname, which is Smith.

- g stands for given name, which is Mary.

There are other possible attributes that can be used in an O/R address, but these are the most common ones when implementing X.400 messaging within an Exchange organization.

SMTP

Simple Mail Transfer Protocol (SMTP) is the standard email transport system for the Internet and is based on the hierarchical Domain Name System (DNS). For the preceding example, Mary Smith's automatically generated SMTP address would be

```
marys@toronto.samplecorp.com
```

assuming that SampleCorp is registered as part of the .com domain.

MS Mail

Microsoft Mail 3.x mail systems use a straightforward addressing scheme based on the format

```
network_name/postoffice_name/mailbox_name
```

where

- network_name is identified by Exchange with the organization name.

- postoffice_name is identified by Exchange with the site name.

- `mailbox_name` is identified by Exchange with the user's mailbox name.

For Mary Smith, her automatically generated MS Mail address would be

```
SAMPLECORP\TORONTO\MARYS
```

Note that each field is limited here to 10 characters.

Lotus cc:Mail

If the Connector for cc:Mail is installed in your organization, exchange also will automatically generate a cc:Mail address for each recipient. For Mary Smith, this cc:Mail address would look like this:

```
Smith, Mary at Toronto
```

Routing

Why so many different types of addresses for each object? It all has to do with how Exchange routes messages between servers, sites, and mail systems. *Routing* is the process by which Exchange transports messages from one point to another. Let's take a look at the various ways messages can be delivered by Exchange.

Routing on the Same Server

Remember that Exchange mailboxes each have a home server, that is, the server in whose Private Information Store the mailbox contents are stored. If a recipient on an Exchange server sends a message to another recipient on the *same* server, the Information Store service uses the destination recipient's distinguished name (DN) to route the message to the destination recipient's mailbox. Other exchange services, such as the Message Transfer Agent (MTA), are not involved in the process, nor are the other types of email addresses of the destination recipient.

Routing within a Site

If the destination recipient is homed on a different server in the *same* site, the Message Transfer Agent (MTA) uses the destination recipient's distinguished name (DN) to route the message to the

Information Store service on the destination recipient's home server, which then moves the message to the destination recipient's mailbox.

Routing to Other Sites or Mail Systems

This is where it gets interesting. Messages sent to recipients in other sites or in foreign mail systems must be delivered by connectors. A typical Exchange organization may use a combination of Site Connectors, Dynamic RAS Connectors, Internet Mail Service Connectors, and other connectors for establishing connectivity between sites connected together using permanent high-speed T-1 lines and dial-up modem connections or to establish connectivity with legacy MS Mail systems, foreign X.400 systems, or external messaging systems such as the Internet or an X.400 messaging system. When you send a message to one of these sites or mail systems, Exchange must determine what routes can be used to route the message and in which order to attempt these routes.

A specific route to another site or mail system is called an *address space* in Exchange terminology. Each connector has one or more address spaces associated with it, which are defined using the Address Space or Connected Sites property sheets. A connector's address space identifies the type of recipient addresses that can be routed through the connector. Address spaces thus can be used to control whether messages from a given organization, site, or location are able to use the connector.

The address space for a connector must be defined when you create the connector and can be specified using the Address Space tab of the connector's property sheet. This tab is common to all Exchange connectors no matter what their type. Figure 10-1 shows the address space for a Site Connector, showing the X.400 address of the connected site. In other words, we are looking at the Toronto site of this particular Site Connector, and the X.400 address listed allows X.400 messages to be routed to the Vancouver site. The scope of the address space indicates that messages sent from anywhere in the Exchange organization can be routed through this connector. The scope for a Site Connector can also be restricted to routing messages sent only from the initial site or from the initial location. Select Edit to modify the existing address of the remote site or New to create additional addresses for the connector's address space.

Exchange combines all the defined address spaces in an organization into a table called the *Gateway Routing Table* (GWART). The

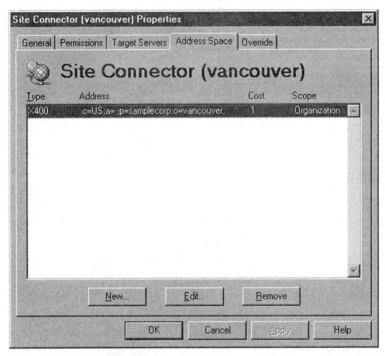

Figure 10-1 The Address Space tab, common to the property sheets of all Exchange connectors.

MTA looks at the GWART to determine which connectors can be used to deliver a message to a destination recipient. The MTA looks at each line (address space) in the GWART that matches the type of address used for the destination recipient. If more than one connector can be used to route a message, the MTA then goes through a specific and somewhat complicated selection process to determine in which order to attempt each connector. If no connectors can be found in the GWART that can route the message to its destination address, a nondelivery report (NDR) is returned.

NOTE

We won't look at all the details of the process by which the MTA selects connectors, but one aspect you should know about is the cost of the connector. Cost values are shown in the GWART. Generally, connectors with lower cost values are attempted before connectors with higher cost values.

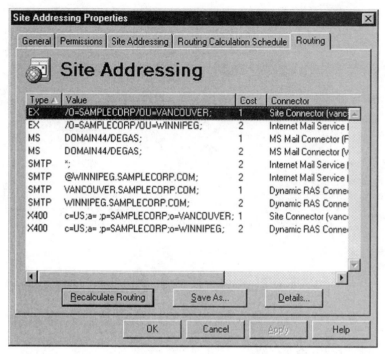

Figure 10-2 The Gateway Routing Table (GWART) for SampleCorp.

Figure 10-2 shows an example of a GWART for SampleCorp. We won't look at all the details of the GWART, but note first the different types of addresses shown in the first column:

- EX stands for Exchange, and refers to the distinguished name (DN) addressing scheme used internally by Exchange. These routes are used only if the destination recipient exists in the Exchange directory and thus has a DN. If you are sending email to a recipient in a foreign mail system using a one-off address, for example, the MTA would ignore EX entries in the GWART when determining how to route the message to its destination.

- MS stands for Microsoft Mail, while SMTP stands for Internet mail. Both these address space types are referred to as *Domain Defined Attribute* (DDA) *format addresses*. This is the format used by Exchange for addresses of Custom Recipients.

- X400 stands for the O/R addresses that are automatically generated for recipients.

Now that we are familiar with Exchange addressing and routing methods, the rest of this chapter examines the various connectors that can be used to establish messaging connectivity with other sites in your organization and with foreign mail systems. We won't look at all the configuration options of these connectors; instead, we will skip the obvious and focus only on what is important or obscure.

Connections Container

First, we should note that the various connectors installed on Exchange servers in an organization are contained within the Connections container in the Exchange directory hierarchy (Fig. 10-3). This container has no interesting properties, so we won't consider it any further.

Site Connector

Site Connectors can only be used to connect different sites in the same Exchange organization together for messaging connectivity. They *cannot* be used to establish messaging connectivity with foreign mail systems or other Exchange organizations.

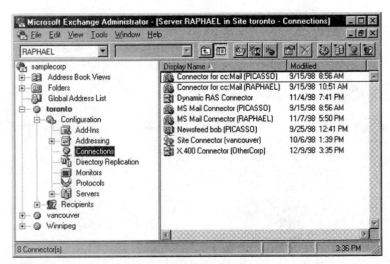

Figure 10-3 The Connections container holds the various connectors installed within an organization.

In fact, the Site Connector is the simplest and most efficient way to connect Exchange sites together for messaging connectivity. Site Connectors require a permanent high-speed LAN or WAN connection between the two sites, since they use remote procedure calls (RPCs) to transport messages between sites.

A Site Connector essentially establishes a direct connection between an Exchange server in the local site and a server in the remote site. Like all Exchange connectors, both ends of the connector must be created and configured for messaging to take place using the connector. With the Site Connector this requirement is simple—when you finish configuring the local side of the connector, a dialog box appears asking you if you want Exchange to automatically create and configure the remote side of the connector in the other site.

The *target servers list* shown in Figure 10-4 lists the names of the Exchange servers available in the remote site for accepting connection attempts from the local site. When a message needs to be

Figure 10-4   The Site Connector property sheet, showing a list of target servers for the remote site.

routed through the Site Connector to the remote site, the connector tries to establish an RPC connection to each of the servers in the target servers list, one at a time, until a connection can be established and the message routed. Target servers with lower *costs* are attempted more frequently. If you have two target servers, each with the same cost, connection attempts will be load balanced between the two target servers.

On the General tab you also can specify whether the Site Connector can use any server in the local site to try to establish a connection to the remote site or whether a specific bridgehead server will be designated for the local site. A *bridgehead server*, if configured, is the only server in the local site that can be used by the Site Connector for initiating a connection with target servers in the remote site. If you have a lot of traffic between sites in your organization, it is a good idea to dedicate one server in your site as a bridgehead server to other sites.

Dynamic RAS Connector

If you don't have a permanent high-speed LAN or WAN connection between some of the sites in your Exchange organization, you can use the Dynamic RAS Connector together with the Windows NT Remote Access Service (RAS) to establish dial-up messaging connectivity between sites. You might use this, for example, to connect a remote branch office to headquarters using an asynchronous device such as a modem, ISDN terminal adapter, or X.25 Packet Assembler/Disassembler (PAD), especially if the messaging traffic is low and a certain amount of messaging latency (delay) is acceptable for users. The Dynamic RAS Connector is also useful as a backup connection between sites, in case the permanent network link goes down causing the Site Connector to fail.

The Dynamic RAS Connector can be scheduled to deliver mail to other sites in different ways (Fig. 10-5):

- *Always* causes the connector to initiate a dial-up networking (DUN) connection to the remote site whenever there is an outbound message waiting in the local MTA queue. You would only use this if message traffic is low, but message latency cannot be tolerated.

- *Selected Times* can be used to schedule DUN connections to the

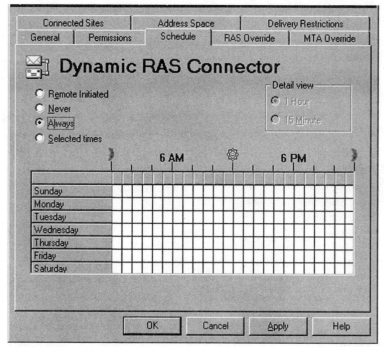

Figure 10-5 The Dynamic RAS Connector property sheet, showing the Schedule tab.

remote site at selected times specified in hourly or 15-minute increments.

- *Remote Initiated* causes the local side of the Dynamic RAS Connector never to initiate a DUN connection to the remote site. Instead, it waits for the remote site to connect to it, whereupon messages waiting in queues are sent both ways.

- *Never* disables the connector.

Other tabs of interest on this property sheet:

- *General* lets you specify the remote MTA transport stack and the DUN phone book entries the connector will use. You must create an MTA Transport Stack for RAS and at least one DUN phonebook entry *before* installing a Dynamic RAS Connector in your site.

- *RAS Override* can be used to supply the Windows NT domain name and credentials to be used by your DUN connection if the remote server is in a different Windows NT domain.

- *MTA Override* can be used to override the settings in the Messaging Defaults tab of the MTA Site Configuration object's property sheet in your site. See Chapter 4 for details.

- *Connected Sites* shows the remote sites that are connected directly to your local site using the Dynamic RAS Connector. This enables directory replication to take place with the remote sites.

- *Delivery Restrictions* lets you accept or reject outbound messages according to who sends them.

X.400 Connector

X.400 Connectors can be used for two purposes:

- For connecting sites together in your Exchange organization. We will consider this scenario below.

- For establishing messaging connectivity with a foreign X.400 mail system or another Exchange organization. In this case, you need to work together with the administrators of the foreign X.400 mail system so that your X.400 Connector and their remote Message Transfer Agent (MTA) can be configured properly to enable messaging to take place.

Why would you use the X.400 Connector instead of the Site Connector for connecting your organization's sites together? The main advantages are that with the X.400 connector you can

- Schedule when and how often intersite messaging connections will be established

- Limit the maximum size of messages that can be sent between sites

The downside of an X.400 Connector is that the server on which it is installed is automatically considered a bridgehead server. This is different from the Site Connector, where you have a choice of whether to specify a local bridgehead server or allow any server in your site to initiate connections with the remote site. If messaging traffic volume is high, your X.400 bridgehead server could become a bottleneck for intersite messaging.

TIP

Here's a planning issue. Say you have three sites A, B, and C connected together using X.400 connectors. How should you configure directory replication to occur between these sites? By having A replicate with B, B with C, and C with A? This uses unnecessary bandwidth. Simply have A replicate with both B and C, and this will do the job most efficiently. To configure the Directory Replication object, see Chapter 4 again.

Another disadvantage is that the X.400 Connector only works with certain kinds of network transports. These supported transport stacks are TCP/IP, TP4, and X.25. Therefore, if you are using IPX/SPX, then X.400 is not an option. Prior to installing your X.400 Connector, you also must install the appropriate transport stack. Even if you have TCP/IP installed on your network, you still need to install a TCP/IP Transport Stack for your X.400 bridgehead servers.

Some of the tabs of interest on this property sheet include

- *Stack.* This is where you specify the transport address information of the X.400 Connector or remote MTA to which you are connecting. The form of this property page depends on the type of transport stack installed. For TCP/IP (Fig. 10-6), you can specify the IP address or DNS host name of the remote machine. The other information here may be used when connecting to foreign X.400 mail systems.

- *General.* This lets you specify the name and password of the other end of the connector. If you are connecting to a foreign mail system, this is the name and password of the foreign MTA. If you are connecting to another site in your organization, the name and password can be found on the General tab of the Message Transfer Agent object's property sheet on the remote server. See Chapter 5 for more details.

- *Schedule* lets you schedule messaging connections through the connector, just as with the Dynamic RAS Connector discussed earlier.

- *Override* can be used to override the settings in the Messaging Defaults tab of the MTA Site Configuration object's property sheet in your site. See Chapter 4 for details.

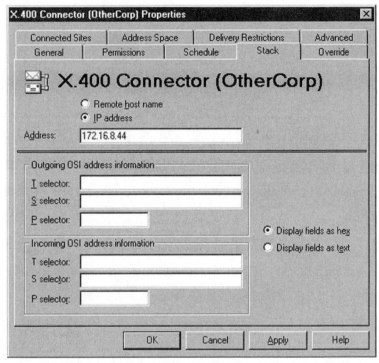

Figure 10-6   The X.400 Connector property sheet, showing the IP address of the remote X.400 Connector.

- *Advanced* lets you configure the maximum message size that can be routed by the connector, plus some other advanced settings for twiddling connections with foreign X.400 mail systems.

- *Connected Sites and Delivery Restrictions* were discussed in the preceding section.

MS Mail Connector and Dirsync

MS Mail Connector

The MS Mail Connector is used to allow messages to be exchanged between your organization and legacy Microsoft Mail 3.x networks (Fig. 10-7). The MS Mail Connector works over LAN, asynchronous (modem), and X.25 network connections and is available in two flavors: PC and AppleTalk.

Microsoft Mail 3.x is an older Microsoft messaging system that works on the store-and-forward model. Clients connect to a

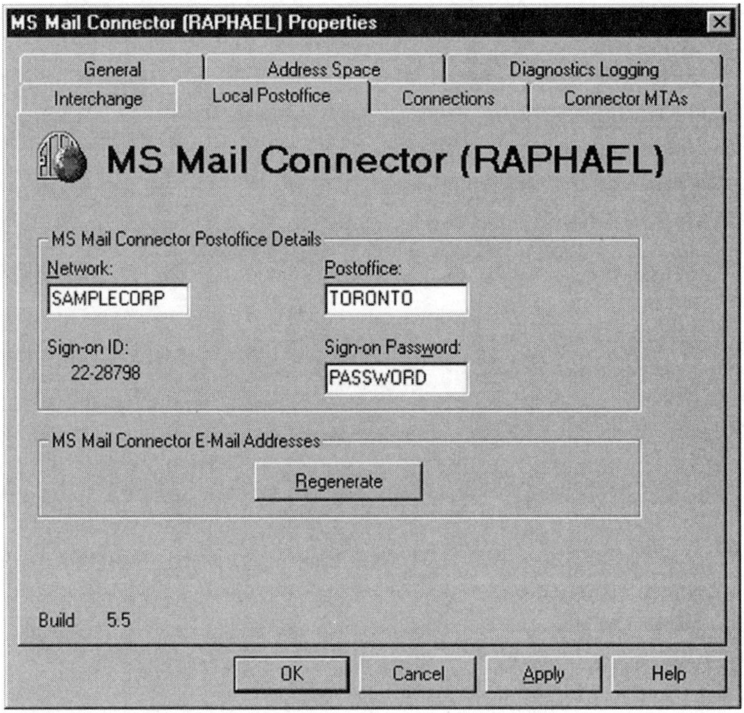

Figure 10-7   The MS Mail Connector.

Postoffice to send and receive mail. This Postoffice is nothing more than a set of special folders on a file server. The Postoffice in MS Mail is a passive entity—all the message processing is done by the clients. Messages are transferred between Postoffices by the MS Mail External program, which essentially acts as a Message Transfer Agent (MTA). Messages also can be routed between Postoffices and *gateways,* which allows messages to be sent to external mail systems such as PROFS or SNADS or to the Internet using the MS Mail SMTP Gateway.

When configuring messaging connectivity between an Exchange organization and an MS Mail system, both sides need to be configured properly. We will only look at the Exchange side of the connection, namely, the MS Mail Connector.

Some of the tabs of interest on this property sheet include

- *Local Postoffice* is the MS Mail address of a temporary Postoffice created on the Exchange server on which the MS Mail Connector is installed. This temporary Postoffice is used for processing mail in transit through the connector and identifies the Exchange server to the Microsoft Mail 3.x messaging system (remember, from the point of view of the remote MS Mail Postoffices, the Exchange server on which the MS Mail Connector is configured must look like just another MS Mail Postoffice).

- *General* lets you configure a maximum message size that can be routed through the connector.

- *Diagnostic Logging* specifies which kinds of MS Mail-related events are logged to the Application Log for viewing with Event Viewer.

- *Interchange* is where you configure the MS Mail Connector Interchange Service, the Windows NT service on the Exchange server responsible for routing messages between the Exchange server and its temporary Local Postoffice. Another Windows NT service, the MS Mail Connector MTA Service, is then responsible for routing messages between the Local Postoffice and remote MS Mail Postoffices. Here is where you specify an administrator mailbox for your Local Postoffice, enable message tracking, and do other stuff.

- *Connections* shows the remote MS Mail Postoffices currently connected. You also can view messages waiting in the message queue and delete them or return them to sender.

- *Connector MTAs* configures the MS Mail Connector MTA Service described earlier. You need to configure a separate instance of this service (i.e., a separate Connector MTA) for each remote MS Mail Postoffice to which you are connecting.

Directory Synchronization

Dirsync stands for directory synchronization. Remember that *directory replication* refers to the exchange of directory information between all servers within an Exchange organization. *Directory synchronization* means something different: the exchange of directory information between a Microsoft Exchange organization and a Microsoft Mail 3.x mail system. For simplicity, we will refer to this process here as *dirsync* instead of directory synchronization.

The way dirsync works in a Microsoft Mail system is this: Each Postoffice in an MS Mail messaging system functions as a Directory Requestor Postoffice, except for one that functions as a Directory Server Postoffice.

A Directory Requestor Postoffice periodically checks to see if the Global Address List (GAL) on its server has changed. If there are any address changes, it sends these changes to the Directory Server Postoffice and requests any additional address changes that the Server Postoffice might have. By changes to the GAL, we mean modifications to any information about recipients in the GAL, such as their email address, telephone number, department, or whatever else is stored concerning them in the MS Mail or Exchange directories. We also mean the addition of new recipients or the deletion of obsolete ones.

The Directory Server Postoffice collects all address changes sent to it by Directory Requestor Postoffices on the MS Mail network and distributes these changes back to the Requestor Postoffices. The Directory Server Postoffice acts as the central clearinghouse for changes to the GAL, making sure that all MS Mail Postoffice servers have up-to-date addressing information for all MS Mail users.

This dirsync process for Microsoft Mail is a scheduled process that makes use of MS Mail messages to exchange addressing updates between the Server Postoffice and the Requestor Postoffices. In a typical MS Mail network, each Requestor Postoffice might send its update message to the Server Postoffice once per day.

For a Microsoft Exchange organization to synchronize its GAL with that of a Microsoft Mail network, the same basic mechanisms must be used. To make this possible, there are several additional components that can be installed on Exchange servers:

- *Dirsync Requestor.* When this component is installed on an Exchange server, this server can act as a Directory Requestor Postoffice as far as an MS Mail network is concerned. In other words, a Dirsync Requestor periodically checks with the Exchange server on which it is installed to see if there are any updates to the Exchange organization's GAL. If changes are found, the Dirsync Requestor uses the MS Mail Connector to send these updates to an MS Mail Directory Server Postoffice according to the specified schedule. If the Server Postoffice has any additional changes, it returns these to the Dirsync Requestor on the Exchange server, and these changes then propagate throughout the Exchange organization. In this scenario you might have one MS Mail Server Postoffice receiving and distributing GAL updates from three MS Mail Requestor

Postoffices and one Exchange server with a Dirsync Requestor installed on it.

- *Dirsync Server.* When this component is installed on an Exchange Server, this server can act as a Directory Server Postoffice as far as an MS Mail network is concerned. In other words, MS Mail Directory Requestor Postoffices periodically check with the servers on which they are installed to see if there are any updates to the MS Mail system's GAL. If changes are found, each Requestor Postoffice sends these updates to a Microsoft Exchange server with a Dirsync Server installed on it according to the specified schedule. If the Exchange server has any additional changes, it returns these to each Requestor Postoffice on the MS Mail network. In this scenario, you might have one Exchange server with a Dirsync Server installed on it receiving and distributing GAL updates from a group of MS Mail Requestor Postoffices.

> **NOTE**
> Things can get more complicated than this, obviously! One thing to note, however, is that an Exchange server can have a Dirsync Server installed or a Dirsync Requestor installed—but not both. Even if there are two different legacy MS Mail networks in your company, an Exchange server can't participate in dirsync with more than one MS Mail network at a time.

- *Remote Dirsync Requestor.* When you want an Exchange server to handle MS Mail directory synchronization by having a Dirsync Server installed on it, you must configure the Exchange server to replace the existing MS Mail Directory Server Postoffice computer. In order to do this, you must create a Remote Dirsync Requestor for each MS Mail Directory Requestor Postoffice on the MS Mail network. For example, if you want your Exchange server to perform dirsync for an MS Mail network consisting of one Directory Server Postoffice and three Directory Requestor Postoffice computers, you configure your Exchange server to replace the Directory Server Postoffice by installing the Dirsync Server component on it, and then you install three Remote Dirsync Requestor components on your Exchange server, one configured for each of the three Directory Requestor Postoffices in the MS Mail network.

■ *Directory Synchronization.* Finally, once you have all the MS Mail
Connector, Dirsync Servers, Dirsync Requestors, and Remote
Dirsync Requestors installed and configured on your Exchange
servers (pretty much in that order), you still need to configure
one more component on the server: the Directory Synchronization object contained within the Server container discussed previously (Fig. 10-8). This will be discussed in a moment.

> **NOTE**
> Everything depends on the MS Mail Connector. If this
> fails, all the other Exchange components used to establish
> dirsync with MS Mail systems will fail to work. This is so
> because they all depend on the MS Mail Connector for establish-
> ing messaging connectivity between Exchange sites and MS Mail
> systems.

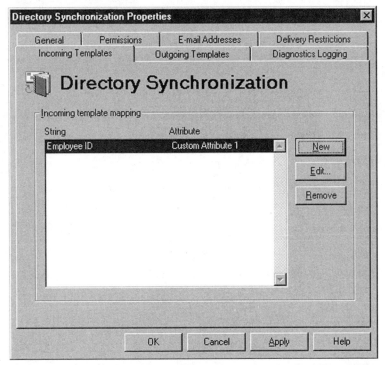

Figure 10-8 Creating a template mapping for the Directory Synchronization
object.

First, instead of tiring you out with more property sheets for the various Dirsync objects, let's just summarize some of the important things you need to configure for these Dirsync Servers, Requestors, and Remote Requestors:

- *Schedule (Dirsync Server and Dirsync Requestor objects).* When dirsync messages are sent by the object.

- *Import Container (Dirsync Requestor and Remote Dirsync Requestor objects).* Which recipient container will receive any address changes imported from the MS Mail Directory Server Postoffice or Exchange Dirsync server.

- *Export Containers (Dirsync Requestor and Remote Dirsync Requestor objects).* Which recipient containers will have their recipients' address information exported to the MS Mail Directory Server Postoffice or Exchange Dirsync server.

- *Trust Level (Dirsync Requestor and Remote Dirsync Requestor objects).* For import containers, setting a trust level assigns this trust level to imported directory information. For export containers, setting a trust level limits what will be exported to recipients whose trust level is less than or equal to the value specified here. Essentially using trust levels lets you control which Exchange recipients are exported to the MS Mail system when dirsync occurs.

> **NOTE**
>
> If you have an Exchange server configured as a Dirsync Server, you can *force* dirsync to occur with MS Mail Directory requestor Postoffices by using the Services utility in Control Panel on the Exchange server to pause and then restart the Directory Synchronization service. Ignore the error message.

The final step in configuring dirsync to occur between an Exchange organization and a Microsoft Mail system is to configure the properties of the Directory Synchronization object on a server in your site. This should be a different server from the ones you have installed Dirsync Requestors or Servers on.

You shouldn't need to configure this object really, the default settings probably will work. The only thing you may want to consider is if you want to exchange extended information about recipients between the two systems. Microsoft Mail uses something called *templates* to record extended information about its recipients. This extended information could be things such as Employee ID numbers, Social Security Numbers, and so on. You can use the Templates tabs on the Directory Synchronization object's property sheet to map this extended information into specified attributes of Exchange recipients within the Exchange directory database, such as the Custom Attributes discussed in Chapters 4 and 6.

Connector for cc:Mail

Briefly, the Connector for cc:Mail enables you to establish messaging connectivity between your Exchange organization and a foreign cc:Mail messaging system and to exchange information in the Exchange Global Address List with the Lotus cc:Mail directory server. One thing to note is that you need to install two Lotus cc:Mail programs on your Exchange server to get this to work: the cc:Mail `Export.exe` and `Import.exe` programs. These two programs provide the interface between the Connector for cc:Mail and a cc:Mail post office. 'Nuff said!

Where Do We Go from Here?

In the next chapter we will look at two connectors not considered in this chapter, the *Internet Mail Service* and the *Internet News Service*. We also will consider more generally the various *Internet protocols* supported by Exchange and how to configure these protocols.

For Review

1. What are connectors used for?
2. Which connectors can be used for intersite messaging? For messaging with foreign mail systems?
3. What types of email addresses are automatically created for new recipients?
4. What is a *distinguished name* (DN)? Give an example.
5. What is an *O/R address*? Describe the commonly defined attributes in such an address when used by Exchange.

6. Describe the format of these types of addresses:

   - MS Mail
   - SMTP
   - Lotus cc:Mail

7. Describe how Exchange routes messages sent

   - To a different mailbox on the same server
   - To a different server in the same site
   - To a different site or foreign mail system

8. What is the GWART, and what is it used for?

9. Explain the term *address space*. Give an example.

10. How are cost values important when Exchange is selecting a connector for routing messages to a different site or foreign mail system.

11. What container holds the connectors installed in an organization?

12. What is the Site Connector used for? Does it have any requirements?

13. Why might you configure a bridgehead server for a Site Connector?

14. What does the list of target servers signify for a Site Connector?

15. When would you use a Dynamic RAS Connector? What are the requirements for it to be used?

16. What scheduling options are there for the Dynamic RAS Connector?

17. When might you configure the RAS Override property page?

18. What can the X.400 Connector be used for? What are the requirements for it to be used?

19. What are the advantages and disadvantages of using an X.400 Connector in place of a Site Connector?

20. What is a *transport stack?*

21. What object must you create and configure to establish messaging between an Exchange organization and a Microsoft Mail 3.x mail system?

22. What additional objects would you need to create and configure to establish directory synchronization (dirsync) between the two systems in the preceding question?

23. Describe how an MS Mail system works.

24. What is the Local Postoffice on an Exchange server that has the MS Mail Connector installed? What two Windows NT services interact with the Local Postoffice?

25. Explain the difference between a Dirsync Server, a Dirsync Requestor, and a Remote Dirsync Requestor. Describe also how they are used.

26. What are *import containers* and *export containers?*

27. What are *trust levels,* and how are they used?

28. What are *templates* and *template mappings?*

29. What two Lotus programs are needed if you want to configure messaging between an Exchange organization and a cc:Mail system?

CHAPTER 11

The Internet

This chapter looks at how Microsoft Exchange supports standard Internet protocols and services, including sending and receiving SMTP email and reading and posting to USENET newsgroups. Topics covered include

- Internet protocols
- Configuring protocols
- Internet Mail Service
- Internet News Service
- Firewalls and security
- Where do we go from here?
- For review

Internet Protocols

The Internet is the worldwide TCP/IP internetwork that grew out of the ARPANET project of the U.S. Department of Defense in the 1970s. The Internet rightly can be considered the "network of networks," and its importance to business, commerce, and communications has grown rapidly in the last few years.

Microsoft Exchange supports the most popular Internet protocols, including DNS, SMTP, POP3, IMAP4, MIME, S/MIME, NNTP, LDAP, HTTP, and SSL. We will briefly look here at the nature and function of each protocol and how it is implemented in Exchange. Then we will see how to configure these protocols for Exchange.

DNS

The *Domain Name System,* or *DNS,* is a worldwide hierarchical naming scheme that allows dotted names to be used to refer to computers on the Internet instead of numeric IP addresses. Using DNS, computers on the Internet can be given friendly, easily remembered names such as

```
vangogh.vancouver.samplecorp.com
```

instead of trying to remember them as numeric IP addresses like

```
172.16.8.200
```

Space doesn't permit us to go into a full treatment of DNS here—any good book on Windows NT will cover this, including the related study guide in this series. All you really need to remember is that client computers connected to the Internet use DNS Servers to resolve DNS host names (more properly called *Fully Qualified Domain Names,* like the one shown above) into IP addresses so that network communication can take place over the Internet.

SMTP

Simple Mail Transfer Protocol, or *SMTP,* is the protocol used on the Internet to send and receive email messages. Exchange supports SMTP through the Internet Mail Service, an installable connector for Exchange. Using the SMTP protocol, one SMTP host can send email to another SMTP host. An *SMTP host* is any computer connected to the Internet and running an SMTP service or *daemon* (the Unix equivalent of a Windows NT service, which runs in the background continually to perform some function). The term *host* refers here to any computer running TCP/IP that is connected to the Internet, although this term is used more commonly in the Unix world than in the Windows world.

SMTP hosts communicate with each other by first establishing a session using TCP port number 25. SMTP hosts then use a series of simple commands such as helo, mail from, rcpt to, data, and quit to initiate the sending and receiving of messages. To troubleshoot an SMTP host, you can use a Telnet client to connect to the host on port 25 and manually type these commands and examine how the host responds.

What is important to realize is that SMTP has no provision for the creation of personal mailboxes. SMTP is simply a mechanism for moving mail from one SMTP host to another. Furthermore, for SMTP to work, an SMTP host needs to be continuously connected to the Internet. If the host is down when mail is coming in, the mail will bounce. Now this was fine in the early days when the Internet consisted of a few thousand high-powered computers continually on-line, but what about today, when there are millions of computers on the Internet, most of them PCs or laptops that dial up occasionally to collect their mail? That is where two other Internet protocols, POP3 and IMAP4, come in.

POP3

Post Office Protocol version 3, or *POP3,* is an Internet protocol supported by Exchange that describes how to implement a maildrop service that can hold mail received through SMTP at a POP3 server until an agent (client program or computer) can call in to collect it. The POP3 server can be a different machine than the SMTP host, or both services can be installed on the same machine as in the case of Exchange. The SMTP service sends and receives the mail, and the POP3 service puts received mail into a mailbox and holds it there until it is retrieved by the user. POP3 also includes authentication methods so that users can only access the mailbox that contains mail intended for them. This allows multiple users to privately access SMTP mail received by a single SMTP host.

POP3 clients such as Microsoft Outlook Express communicate with POP3 servers by establishing a session using TCP port number 110 to retrieve messages from their mailbox. To send a message, POP3 clients use SMTP on port 25. POP3 clients and servers use a series of simple commands such as user, pass, stat, list, retr, and quit to download messages from their mailbox.

One disadvantage of POP3 is that when a user connects to retrieve his or her mail, he or she must download *all* of it. POP3 doesn't let users leave their mail on the server. This can be a problem for a user who uses more than one computer to access his or her mail, such as someone who accesses his or her mail using a PC at work and using a laptop when traveling. This problem is solved by using the IMAP4 protocol.

IMAP4

Internet Mail Access Protocol version 4 revision 1, or *IMAP4rev1,* is an Internet protocol supported by Exchange that expands on the functionality of POP3. Like POP3, IMAP4 is used to allow IMAP4 clients to retrieve their SMTP mail from an IMAP-compliant server. IMAP4 is used only to retrieve mail—SMTP is still used to send it.

IMAP4 incorporates all the features of POP3 plus these additional enhancements:

- Users can choose which mail they want to download from the server and leave the rest.

- Users can read the headers or a part of a message without downloading the entire message.

- Users can create a hierarchical collection of folders on the server for storing and classifying their messages.

- Users can search for messages on the server based on information in the header, subject, or body of the message.

IMAP4 clients such as Microsoft Outlook Express communicate with IMAP4 servers by establishing a session using TCP port number 143 to retrieve messages from their mailbox. To send a message, IMAP4 clients use SMTP on port 25. IMAP4 clients and servers use a series of simple commands such as `login`, `select`, `fetch`, `store`, `list`, and `close` to download messages from their mailbox.

NOTE

POP3 and IMAP4 as implemented on Exchange support the following user authentication methods:

- *Basic Authentication.* Password is transmitted as clear text. Supported by almost all mail client software, Microsoft or otherwise.

- *Windows NT Challenge/Response.* Also called *NTLM,* a secure authentication method in which a user's password is not actually transmitted over the network. This method is only supported by Windows NT clients, however.
- *Microsoft Commercial Internet Server (MCIS) Membership System.* Used primarily for creating membership lists for anonymous users connecting over the Internet, such as a membership list for an on-line bookstore.
- *Secure Sockets Layer (SSL) protocol.* Encrypts transmissions using public key cryptography. Note that the SSL protocol optionally can be applied *on top of* the other three authentication methods described here. That is, you can have Basic Authentication with SSL or without SSL, and so on. This means that there are $3 \times 2 = 6$ different authentication methods for Internet protocols that are supported by Exchange.

MIME

Multipurpose Internet Mail Extensions, or *MIME,* is a method for sending nontext information using SMTP mail. SMTP originally was designed as a text-only messaging protocol, but early on users saw the advantage of being able to send binary attachments to SMTP messages. These binary files can include image files, sound files, movies, word-processing documents, spreadsheets, executable programs, and so on.

An early method of encoding these binary files so that they could be transmitted as text was Uuencode, which stands for Unix-to-Unix Encoding. In the Macintosh world this was known as BinHex. Uuencode was a simple method of converting binary 8-bit data into ASCII 7-bit data so that it could be sent as text using SMTP.

MIME is an improvement on Uuencode by providing a way of using message headers to indicate the content type of each attachment to a message and multiple encoding methods for different kinds of content. MIME allows email messages to be constructed of several parts, each of which contains data encoded using a different method. MIME enables users to create email messages that contain Rich Text Format (RTF) information, including images, sounds, and other multimedia and binary content. MIME also enables users to create messages using character sets other than the US-ASCII character set. Exchange supports both MIME and Uuencode for sending attachments with messages.

The only important thing to remember is that an attachment must be encoded in such a way that the user at the other end can read it. If you encode a message using MIME but the recipient of the message is using older mail software that only supports Uuencode, he or she won't be able to read your attachment.

S/MIME

Secure Multipurpose Internet Mail Extensions, or *S/MIME,* is an extension to MIME that allows messages and attachments to be encrypted using public key cryptography. This ensures messaging privacy and verification of the sender's identity using digital signatures.

NNTP

Network News Transfer Protocol, or *NNTP,* is an Internet standard protocol supported by Exchange that makes possible the worldwide news and bulletin board system known as *USENET.* The USENET system consists of tens of thousands of newsgroups covering every topic imaginable under the sun. NNTP is a client/server protocol where

- NNTP hosts (servers) replicate newsgroups and their messages to other NNTP hosts around the world using *newsfeeds* (or simply *feeds*).

- NNTP clients connect to an NNTP host to download a list of newsgroups, download messages for a selected newsgroup, and read messages and post new messages to a newsgroup.

NNTP clients such as Microsoft Outlook Express communicate with NNTP servers by establishing a session using TCP port number 119 to download newsgroups and their messages and post new messages to newsgroups. NNTP clients and servers use a series of simple commands such as `list`, `group`, `article`, `post`, and `quit` to download newsgroups, read messages, and post new messages, to newsgroups.

Exchange supports NNTP through the Internet News Service, an installable connector for Exchange.

LDAP

Lightweight Directory Access Protocol, or *LDAP,* is an Internet protocol supported by Exchange that allows LDAP clients such as Microsoft Outlook Express to connect to an X.500-compliant directory service such as the Microsoft Exchange directory to search for, view, add, modify, and delete information contained in the directory, provided the user has the appropriate permissions. X.500 is an International Telecommunications Union (ITU) recommendation for the design and operation of a directory service. The Microsoft Exchange directory database and directory service are modeled after the X.500 recommendations.

As an example, using Outlook Express, you can use LDAP to connect to an Exchange server and view the telephone numbers and other information for recipients created on that server. LDAP provides a kind of white pages access to information about recipients stored in an organization's directory.

LDAP clients such as Outlook Express communicate with X.500-compliant directory servers such as Exchange Server by establishing a session using TCP port number 389 to access directory information on the server. LDAP clients and servers use a series of simple commands such as BindRequest, SearchRequest, ModifyRequest, and AddRequest to search the directory, add new information, view existing information, or delete information from the directory.

LDAP uses the same authentication methods that POP3 and IMAP4 employ.

HTTP

Hypertext Transfer Protocol, or *HTTP,* is the standard Internet protocol for access to the World Wide Web. HTTP is a client/server protocol in which HTTP clients called *Web browsers* send request commands to HTTP servers called *Web servers* using TCP port number 80. The server then responds by sending the client the requested file or document, usually called a *Web page.*

Microsoft Exchange does not in itself support HTTP as a method of transporting information over the Internet, apart from sending SMTP messages in HTML format. However, combined with Microsoft Internet Information Server (IIS) version 3.0 or higher, Exchange supports access to users' mailboxes and to public folders using a component called *Outlook Web Access* that was discussed in Chapter 9.

SSL

Secure Sockets Layer, or *SSL,* protocol is a standard Internet protocol supported by Microsoft Exchange that allows messages to be signed using digital signatures and encrypted using public key cryptography. This allows the recipient of a message to be sure of the sender's identity and ensure the privacy of the communication.

SSL works on top of the other Internet protocols described earlier. For example, SSL can provide secure, encrypted transmission for SMTP messaging. SSL uses a pair of asymmetric keys to encrypt and decrypt messages. The private key is known only to the client program, while the public key is free to anyone to use. SSL signs messages using X.509 digital certificates, which can be validated by a public Certificate Authority (CA) such as Verisign, Inc. This allows recipients to verify the identity of the sender of a message.

In order to use SSL, you need access to a CA who can issue certificates to identify servers and/or clients. You also need to install the Key Manager Server (KM) component on one Exchange server in your organization. This will create two new directory objects called the *Site Encryption Configuration* object and *CA* object that can be used to enable SSL and other advanced forms of security for your organization. There's more to it than this, but we won't worry about the details.

TIP
Pay attention to the version of Microsoft Outlook referred to in your exam questions. Microsoft Outlook 97 (version 8.0.3) supports only SMTP and POP3. Microsoft Outlook 98 (version 8.5) now supports SMTP, POP3, IMAP4, LDAP, NNTP, and S/MIME. Previously, you had to use Microsoft Outlook Express if you wanted to have IMAP4, LDAP, or NNTP functionality.

Configuring Protocols

Exchange allows you to configure certain aspects of the POP3, IMAP4, NNTP, LDAP, and HHTP protocols at three different levels:

- The site Protocols container, located in a site's Configuration container, can be used to configure all five of these protocols at the site level, that is, for all objects within the site (Fig. 11-1).

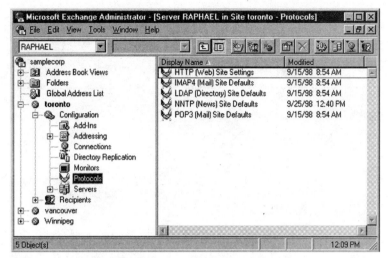

Figure 11-1   The Protocols container for the site Toronto, containing objects used to configure default settings for POP3, IMAP4, NNTP, LDAP, and HTTP at the site level.

For example, you could enable NNTP for any Exchange server in your site using the NNTP object in the Protocols container.

- The server Protocols container, located in each Server container, can be used to override the site defaults set above for POP3, IMAP4, NNTP, or LDAP on a particular Exchange server. You cannot configure HTTP at the server level. For example, you can disable NNTP for a particular Exchange server if it is enabled by default for all servers in the site, as described earlier.

- The property sheet for any Mailbox or Custom Recipient object has a Protocols tab that can be used to override the site and server defaults set earlier for any protocol. For example, you could prevent a particular recipient from using NNTP to connect to USENET using this tab.

Protocols Containers

Using the site- and server-level Protocols containers, you can configure default settings for Internet protocols as follows:

- You can accept or reject connections to your site or server based on the IP address of the remote client (Fig. 11-2). This only works with the POP3, NNTP, and LDAP protocols. This is a good

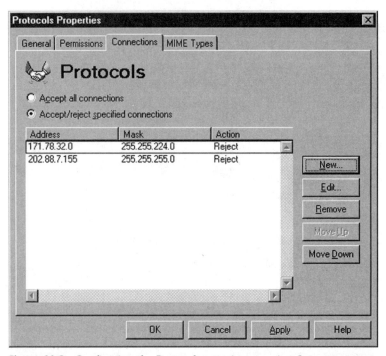

Figure 11-2 Configuring the Protocols container to reject Internet connections by certain IP addresses.

way of blocking out attacks from hackers. You can accept or reject any number of individual IP addresses or IP subnetworks by specifying an IP address and subnet mask.

- You can configure which file extensions will be mapped to MIME types for attachments to incoming messages and what MIME types will be assigned for attachments to outbound messages based on their file extensions. This is used to create a set of mappings between the applications used to create and display attachments and the MIME types used to encode those attachments.

NOTE

If you want to accept or reject HTTP connection attempts to your Outlook Web Access based on the IP address of the remote client, you can do this using the Internet Service Manager tool on the server on which Microsoft Internet Information Server (IIS) is installed.

Table 11-1   Internet Protocol Directory Objects

Protocol	Site Level	Server Level
HTTP	√	
IMAP4	√	√
LDAP	√	√
NNTP	√	√
POP3	√	√

Protocol Objects

There are five protocol directory objects at the site level and four at the server level that can be configured, as shown in Table 11-1. Server-level settings override site-level settings.

You can configure various settings using the property sheets of these protocols. Table 11-2 summarizes some of the configuration options you can specify for each protocol.

> **NOTE**
> The message-encoding settings specify the encoding method to which incoming SMTP messages are converted when a POP3 client connects to Exchange to retrieve his or her mail. Exchange stores incoming messages in native Exchange format, and these messages are then converted to the appropriate format for the client. However, this is only true for messages sent from other users in the organization. If a message comes in from the Internet, Exchange stores it in its native format, and it is not converted.

In addition to the preceding configuration options, some of the protocol objects have more specific settings that can be configured. For example,

- *HTTP.*   You can create public folder shortcuts to allow public folders to be accessed using a standard Web browser through Outlook Web Access. You also can selectively allow anonymous access to anonymous public folders and the Global Address List

Table 11-2 Configuration Options for Protocol Directory Objects at the Site and Server Levels

Configuration Option	HTTP	IMAP4	LDAP	NNTP	POP3
Enable/disable protocol	√	√	√	√	√
Enable client access			√		
Specify authentication method		√	√	√	√
Allow anonymous access	√	√	√	√	
MIME message encoding		√		√	√
Uuencode message encoding				√	√
Support S/MIME signatures				√	
Specify character set		√			√
Use Rich Text Format (RTF)		√			√
Specify TCP port number			√		
Idle time-out		√	√	√	√
Close idle connections		√	√	√	√

and determine how many address list entries are returned to the client.

- *IMAP4.* You can enable fast message retrieval, which causes Exchange to estimate the approximate size of messages on the server instead of determining their correct size. You also can specify a Windows NT account to be used for anonymous access to Exchange by IMAP4 clients.

- *LDAP.* You can configure how LDAP clients can use substrings when searching for information in the Exchange directory (Fig. 11-3) and how many results should be returned per search query. You also can configure Exchange to refer an LDAP client to a different Exchange organization if the desired information cannot be found in the organization's directory.

- *NNTP.* You can view the properties of newsfeeds created on the server and accept or delete NNTP control messages waiting

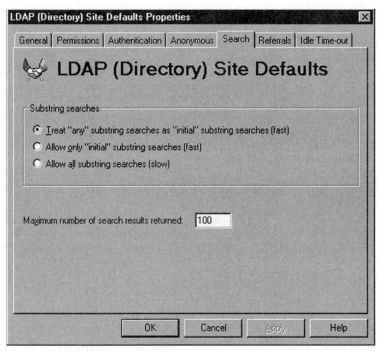

Figure 11-3 Configuring search options for the LDAP protocol at the site level.

in the queue. NNTP control messages are used when one NNTP host replicates with another.

Protocols Tab

Finally, using the Protocols tab on the property sheets for Mailbox and Custom Recipient objects, you can configure how individual recipients interact with Exchange using HTTP, IMAP4, LDAP, NNTP, and POP3 (Fig. 11-4). Table 11-3 shows the configuration options available for these protocols at the recipient level.

Internet Mail Service

The Internet Mail Service is actually a connector similar to the other connectors discussed in Chapter 10 and is implemented on Exchange as a Windows NT service, just as the other connectors

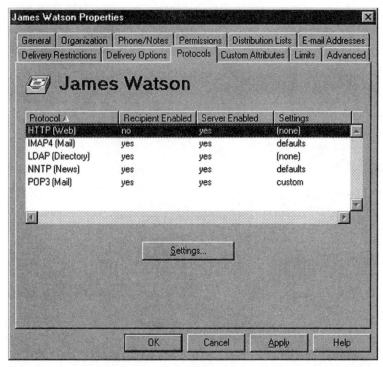

Figure 11-4   Enabling and disabling Internet protocols for a specific Mailbox recipient object.

are. The Internet Mail Service enables Exchange to send and receive SMTP mail over the Internet. In effect, it acts as a gateway between your normal MAPI-based Exchange mail system and the Internet SMTP mail system. Or you could use the Internet Mail Service as your sole messaging service on Exchange, in which case your Exchange server can be considered an SMTP host. Or you could use the Internet Mail Service to connect your Exchange sites together, using the Internet as your backbone network.

Prior to installing the Internet Mail Service on Exchange, you need to do a few things:

- Install TCP/IP. Then configure the DNS host name and domain of your Exchange server and the IP address of the DNS server located at your Internet Service Provider (ISP). You can configure these settings using the Network utility in Control Panel. By

Table 11-3 Configuration Options for Protocol Directory Objects at the Recipient Level

Configuration Option	HTTP	IMAP4	LDAP	NNTP	POP3
Enable/disable protocol	√	√	None	√	√
Use protocol default settings from site and server levels		√		√	
MIME message encoding		√		√	√
Uuencode message encoding				√	√
Specify character set		√			√
Use Rich Text Format (RTF)		√			√
Include all public folders when a folder list is requested		√		√	√
Allow user to act as a delegate		√		√	√

specifying the DNS server you enable your Exchange server to determine the IP address of other SMTP hosts on the Internet, given their fully qualified domain name.

- Have your ISP create A and MX records for your Exchange server on their DNS server. The A record resolves your Exchange server's name into its IP address, whereas the MX record identifies your Exchange server as an SMTP mail exchanger host and specifies which email addresses should be routed to your server.

- Establish network connectivity to your ISP, using either a dedicated, permanent line like a T-1 line or a dial-up connection using Windows NT RAS with an analog modem or ISDN terminal adapter.

NOTE

If your users can send SMTP mail to other people on the Internet but can't receive their replies in return, the DNS records for your Exchange server that runs the Internet Mail Service are probably in error.

The Internet Mail Service is installed and initially configured using a Wizard started by selecting File, New Other, Internet Mail Service from the Exchange Administrator program menu. Once installed, you can find Internet Mail Service's associated directory object in the Connections container for your site and can further configure it by opening its property sheet. Note that you need to use Services in Control Panel to stop and restart the Internet Mail Service after modifying any of the settings on its property sheet.

NOTE

After you install the Internet Mail Service or any other connector, you should run the Microsoft Exchange Performance Optimizer program on your Exchange server.

Let's now look at some of the more important configuration options available on various tabs of the Internet Mail Service property sheet:

- *General.* This specifies maximum message size.

- *Internet Mail* (Fig. 11-5). This configures message encoding for outbound attachments, character sites, S/MIME, message tracking, administrator's mailbox, and other settings related to the sending and receiving of SMTP mail over the Internet.

NOTE

If users in your organization regularly send Internet mail to users outside the organization and these external users complain that the messages your users send come in garbled, try changing the outbound attachments setting here from MIME to Uuencode, since Uuencode is often used for Unix SMTP hosts on the Internet.

Figure 11-5   Configuring the Internet Mail Service.

- *Dial-up Connections.*   This specifies dial-up networking (DUN) phonebook entries and scheduling options.

- *Connections.*   This specifies various connection formats such as

  - *Transfer mode.*   Whether to only accept inbound messages, only send outbound messages, or do both. Click Advanced to specify the maximum number of inbound and outbound connections allowed.

  - *Message Delivery.*   Whether to use DNS to determine which SMTP host to deliver each outbound SMTP message to or to forward all outbound SMTP messages to a specific SMTP host. If you want to enable your users to send SMTP mail to anyone on the Internet, select Use DNS instead of forwarding messages to another host. If you want to be able to send email to an SMTP host that is *not* connected to the Internet (and hence has no DNS name), select the Email Domain button here and specify the host's IP address.

- *Accept Connections.* Whether to accept unauthenticated inbound connections to port 25 from any SMTP host, specify specific hosts you will accept or reject connections from, or force inbound hosts to connect using authentication and/or SSL encryption. Note that if you choose to accept connections from any host, you are opening up your server for exploitation by purveyors of "spam" (mass marketing by junk mail), since your Exchange server can then act as an *SMTP relay agent* that can relay mail from unauthorized users to other DNS domains. As an alternative, you could select the Hosts button here and reject the IP addresses of specific hosts or networks that are sending your users "spam."

- *Address Space.* Use this tab to specify which SMTP addresses your server can process. If you specify * for the address, this means that the Internet mail Service will route any SMTP message it receives. If you want only to route messages for `samplecorp.com` through your server, you would specify `samplecorp.com` as the address here.

- *Routing.* This lets you choose whether or not to reroute incoming SMTP mail. If you choose to do so, this page also lets you specify what to do with incoming SMTP mail. For example, the routing entry

  ```
  toronto.samplecorp.com    <inbound>
  ```

  means that inbound mail of the form recipient@toronto.samplecorp.com will be accepted by the Internet Mail Service and all other inbound mail will be rerouted outbound.

> **NOTE**
> You *must* configure the Internet Mail Service to reroute mail if you want to enable users to send mail to recipients outside your Exchange organization. If you select Do Not Reroute Incoming SMTP Mail, your users will only be able to send SMTP mail to recipients in the Global Address List of your organization.

- *Security.* This configures SSL or Windows NT Challenge/Response security for specific email domains.

- *Queues.* Here you can view details of or delete messages waiting in the inbound and outbound queues for the Internet Mail Service.

NOTE

Consider an Exchange organization called SampleCorp with two sites, Toronto and Vancouver. Users in the Toronto site will by default have SMTP email addresses of the form user@toronto.samplecorp.com, while users in the Vancouver site will have addresses like user@vancouver.samplecorp.com. What if you want to make life easier for your all your users by allowing them to send and receive SMTP email using an address of the simpler form, that is, user@samplecorp.com? In other words, you want to hide the site portion of the DNS domain name for users' email addresses. Here's what you need to do to accomplish this

1. Modify the MX record in the DNS server that is servicing your organization so that it correctly points to your Exchange server running the Internet Mail Service using the samplecorp.com domain designation.

2. Use the Routing tab on the Internet Mail Service property sheet to specify that mail sent to samplecorp.com will be considered inbound mail.

3. Open the Site Addressing tab of the Side Addressing directory object for each site and add an SMTP proxy address of the form @samplecorp.com.

Internet News Service

The Internet News Service enables an Exchange server to act as an NNTP host and participate in the worldwide USENET news system. Using the Internet News Service, an Exchange server can exchange newsfeeds with other NNTP hosts on the Internet and allows NNTP clients such as Outlook Express to connect to and download newsgroups and their messages.

To install and configure the Internet News Service on an Exchange server, you create a Newsfeed on that server using File, New Other, Newsfeed from the Exchange Administrator program menu. This starts a long and somewhat complicated Wizard that we won't go into here. What you need to know is that newsfeeds can be of two types, depending on who initiates the connection:

- *Push feeds* exist when the USENET service provider's NNTP host initiates the connection with your Exchange server and pushes newsgroup information to your server on a schedule determined by the provider. Push feeds are typically used when the newsfeeds are large, such as when you want to download a full USENET newsfeed.

- *Pull feeds* exist when your Exchange server initiates the connection with your provider's NNTP host and pulls selected newsgroup content from the host on a schedule you yourself determine. Pull feeds are used for smaller, select feeds that you want to have control over.

There is another way of classifying newsfeeds, however:

- *Inbound feeds* are received by your Exchange server from a USENET provider's NNTP host.

- *Outbound feeds* are ones you generate and send to your provider's NNTP host. You can create a hierarchy of public folders and send it to your provider in the form of a newsgroup hierarchy.

The bottom line is, when you create a newsfeed, you can specify that it be an

- Inbound pull feed
- Inbound push feed
- Outbound pull feed
- Outbound push feed
- Inbound and outbound pull feed
- Inbound and outbound pull feed

The last two are the usual types created. Use an inbound/outbound push feed only if you have gigabytes and gigabytes of free space on your Exchange server—a full USENET feed nowadays is huge, and contains over 40,000 different newsgroups.

Once a Newsfeed is created, it can be configured by opening its property sheet. Newsfeed objects are located in the Connections container for your site, along with other connectors installed on your site (Fig. 11-6). Like other connectors, newsfeeds are implemented as a Windows NT service called, you guessed it, the Internet News Service.

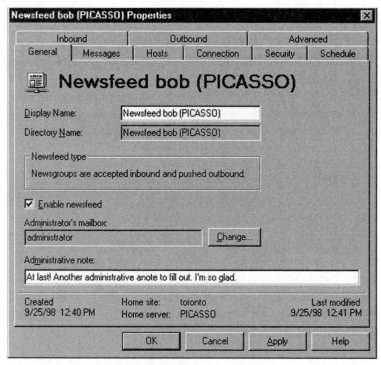

Figure 11-6 Configuring a newsfeed (the Internet News Service).

Let's now look at some of the more important configuration options available on various tabs of a Newsfeed property sheet:

■ *General.* This shows the type of newsfeed you created when you ran the Wizard, and cannot be changed. You also can disable your newsfeed using the checkbox.

■ *Messages.* This lets you specify message size limits for incoming and outgoing messages.

■ *Hosts.* Here you need to specify the site and host names of the remote NNTP host from which you are receiving your USENET feed.

■ *Connection.* This specifies whether you are connecting to the remote NNTP host using a LAN or DUN connection.

■ *Security.* You may need to configure settings here if your provider's NNTP host requires authentication to be accessed.

- *Schedule.* This specifies when and how often you connect to your provider's NNTP host (if you have created a pull feed).

- *Inbound.* If your server receives inbound feeds from your provider, you can specify which newsgroups to receive and have replicated to your server.

- *Outbound.* This lets you specify any Exchange public folders you want to replicate out to your provider's USENET host, if you created an outbound feed.

Firewalls and Security

There's one more topic to consider briefly here. Most networks these days are connected to the Internet through a *firewall,* a program or device whose main purpose is to prevent unauthorized users from accessing the network through its Internet connection. A firewall is like a gateway between your network and the Internet that allows your users to freely access Internet services and resources while preventing access in the opposite direction.

A simple form of firewall is to use a machine with two network interface cards in it. This dual-homed machine acts as a router and separates the network outside (the Internet) from the network inside (your corporate network). All communications between the two networks take place through this machine. Its

Table 11-4 Important Default Port Numbers for Configuring Firewalls for Exchange

Protocol	Port Number	Port Number with SSL
SMTP	25	N/A
POP3	110	995
IMAP4	143	993
NNTP	119	N/A
LDAP	389	636
HTTP	80	443
RPC connectivity	135	N/A

routing table can be configured to block access over certain TCP and UDP ports in certain directions, if it is sophisticated enough to handle this. In addition, proxy software is often installed on the machine that receives packets from one network and then forwards them to the other network while masking the identity of the sending host from the receiving host.

We can't get into a lot of details about firewalls here. What we will point out is that any firewall can be configured to allow or deny packets the right to traverse it based on either the packet's IP address (source or destination) or the TCP or UDP port used by the packet. In this context, it is a good idea if you memorize the standard (default) port numbers for the various Internet protocols and services supported by Exchange, as shown in Table 11-4. Using this table, we can see, for example, that if we want to allow an LDAP client such as Microsoft Outlook Express to connect to an Exchange server to obtain directory information, we need to keep port 389 open on the firewall to allow incoming packets on this port.

NOTE
If you can't connect to an Exchange server on the far side of a router using the Exchange Administrator program, your router is probably configured to block traffic on port number 135. This port must be open between Exchange servers in a site to enable RPC connectivity between them.

Where Do We Go from Here?

In the next chapter we will look at how you can *monitor* Exchange servers and messaging connectivity using Server and Link Monitors. We also will look at monitoring Exchange using the Windows NT administrative tool Performance Monitor.

For Review

1. Describe briefly what each of the following Internet protocols are used for

   - DNS
   - SMTP

- POP3
- IMAP4
- MIME
- S/MIME
- NNTP
- LDAP
- HTTP
- SSL

2. Which of the preceding Internet protocols does Exchange support?

3. Which of the preceding protocols can be configured at
   - The site level
   - The server level
   - The individual recipient level

4. What options can you configure for POP3, IMAP4, LDAP, NNTP, and HTTP at the site and server levels? At the individual recipient level?

5. What can you use the Internet Mail Service for in an Exchange organization?

6. What must you do prior to installing and configuring the Internet Mail Service on an Exchange server?

7. What should you do after installing the Internet Mail Service on an Exchange server?

8. What is an MX record used for?

9. Describe some of the settings you can configure using the Internet Mail Service property sheet.

10. How can you prevent your Exchange server from being used to relay "spam"?

11. How can you make sure that users in your organization can send SMTP mail to anyone on the Internet?

12. Describe some of the settings you can configure using a Newsfeed property sheet.

13. Name and explain the different kinds of newsfeeds supported by Exchange.

14. List the various port numbers of significance when configuring a firewall to protect your Exchange server from hostile attacks by users on the Internet.

CHAPTER 12

Monitoring

This chapter looks at how to monitor the health and status of your Exchange servers using various tools. Topics covered include

- Server monitors
- Link monitors
- Message queues
- Performance monitor
- Where do we go from here?
- For review

Server Monitors

Once your Exchange organization is up and running, you need to monitor its health and status on an ongoing basis to ensure that your implementation is performing the way you expect it to. Exchange provides several tools for doing this, which we will examine in this chapter.

The first tool we will look at is an installable Exchange component called a *Server Monitor*. Server Monitors verify that essential

Exchange services and other Windows NT services are running properly on specified Exchange servers. If services are not functioning, appropriate actions can be taken such as generating a Windows NT administrative alert, sending an email notification to an administrator, restarting, or even rebooting the server. Server Monitors also can be used to check whether an Exchange server's clock is properly synchronized and can reset a clock that is off by a specified amount.

Server Monitors do not require any special permissions to check the status of services on Exchange servers, but they do require RPC connectivity with the servers they are monitoring. Permissions are required, however, if you want the monitor to be able to restart services or computers or reset clocks.

When you create a Server Monitor, it is located in the Monitors container in your site Configuration container. When you create a Server Monitor object, here are some of the things you need to consider when configuring its property sheet:

- *Polling Interval.* A polling interval specifies how frequently the Server Monitor checks the services on the designated Exchange servers. On the General tab you can specify two different polling intervals:
  - *Normal.* This specifies how often the Monitor checks servers that are running properly. The default is every 15 minutes.
  - *Critical.* This is how often the Monitor checks servers that are detected as having a problem, such as when an essential Exchange service stops on the server. The default is every 5 minutes.

- *Escalation Path* (Fig. 12-1). Use the Notification tab to specify what series of notification actions should be taken when a server becomes unstable. You specify a series of actions that should take place and when each action is to occur (the time between the condition being recognized by the monitor and the notification action being performed). Possible notification actions can include

  - Sending an email notification to an administrator
  - Generating a Windows NT alert
  - Running any executable, such as a program to notify a pager

  When you create a notification action, you can specify whether this action should apply to servers that are

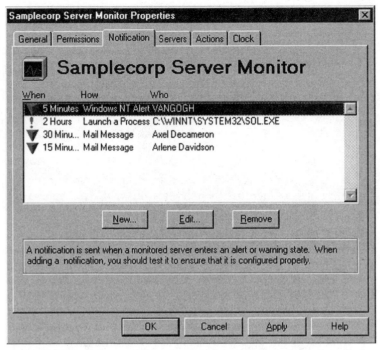

Figure 12-1 Escalation path for a Server Monitor. If all else fails, play solitaire.

- Either in a Warning state or in an Alert state
- In an Alert state only

The meaning of these two states is as follows:

- An *Alert state* (red triangle) means that a serious condition exists: the server is not responding, a service is not working, or the server's clock is way off for some reason.
- A *Warning state* (red exclamation) means that there is only a possible problem: the clock is off slightly or the server has not been checked recently.

- *Servers and Services.*   Use the Servers tab to specify which Exchange services in your organization will be checked using this monitor and which Windows NT services will be monitored on these servers. By default, the Exchange services monitored are the ones associated with the directory, information store, and message transfer agent.

- *Actions.* Use the Actions tab to specify what should be done when the monitor detects that a Windows NT services is not running on the monitored Exchange server. You can select from three different kinds of actions:

  - Do nothing.
  - Attempt to restart the service.
  - Attempt to reboot the server.

  You can configure the monitor to make three attempts to remedy the problem. For example, you could try twice to restart the service, and if that fails, you can try to reboot the server. If you configure the monitor to reboot the server, you should specify a *restart message* here that will appear on the Exchange server's console and a delay time for this message to be displayed before the reboot attempt takes place, to give time to anyone working at the server's console to save their work. Restart the server only as a last resort.

- *Synchronize Clocks.* Use the Clock tab to specify how far the server's clock needs to be off before it is considered being in an Alert state or a Warning state. If you select the checkboxes here, you can cause the monitor to attempt to synchronize the server's clock if it goes into either of these two states.

- *Log File.* You can have the monitor create an additional log file recording the status of the services on the monitored Exchange servers. Use the General tab to configure this option.

Once you configure your new Server Monitor (and you can create several of them if you want to), you need to start it. This can be done two ways:

- *Manual Start.* Select the Server Monitor in the Exchange Administrator program, select an Exchange server to run the monitor, and then choose Start Monitor from the Tools menu. The monitor's status window will open (Fig. 12-2). The status of a monitored Exchange server can be seen immediately by the symbol showing in the first column of the monitor's status window:

  - Green triangle: Everything OK
  - Red exclamation: Warning!
  - Red triangle: Alert!!
  - Blue question mark: Not sure what's happening.

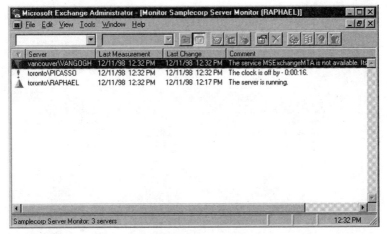

Figure 12-2   The status window for a Server Monitor that is running.

Note that if you close the Exchange Administrator program, the monitor stops running.

- *Automatic Start.*   To automatically start a Server Monitor when the Exchange server is booted, you can create a shortcut to the Exchange Administrator program `admin.exe` using the `/m` switch:

```
/m site_name\monitor_name\server_name
```

starts the Exchange Administrator program and runs the specified Monitor using the specified Exchange server. Then you can place this shortcut in the Startup program group so that it will start automatically when the administrator logs on to the server. Finally, you can configure a Windows NT AutoAdminLogon registry setting to have the server automatically logon using the administrator account when a reboot occurs. Make sure you have your server securely locked away if you plan to use this feature!

If you observe in the monitor's status window that a monitored Exchange server is in a problem state, you can double-click on the server's name to open a property sheet that gives more information about the problem. For the selected server, this property sheet displays (Fig. 12-3):

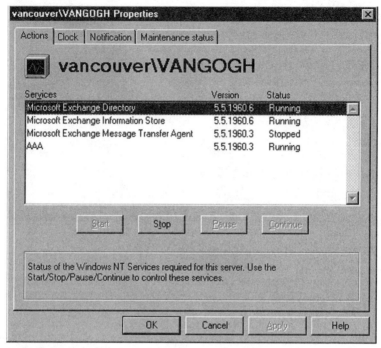

Figure 12-3 Looking deeper into the status of a monitored server.

- The status and version of monitored services. You also can start, stop, pause, and continue services here
- Information about the settings of the server's clock
- What notifications have already been sent automatically concerning the problem
- The maintenance status of the monitored server

NOTE

If you are going to perform scheduled maintenance on an Exchange server, you should run the admin.exe command with the appropriate /t switch options prior to taking the server offline. This puts the server into maintenance mode and stops monitoring actions for the server (so the monitor won't get confused and think the server is in a problem state). The various options for the /t switch are:

- /t n puts the server into maintenance mode and stops notifications from being generated by monitors, but if the monitor wants to initiate a repair actions (like trying to restart a stopped service), it will do so.
- /t r puts the server into maintenance mode and allows monitors to generate notifications concerning the state of the server but stops them from initiating any repair actions.
- /t nr puts the server into maintenance mode and stops monitors from either generating notifications or initiating repair actions concerning the server (preferred).
- /t takes the server out of maintenance mode into normal mode again.

You can remember this /t switch as "t"ake the server off-line for maintenance!

Link Monitors

Link Monitors verify that messaging is functioning between Exchange servers in your organization and between your organization and a foreign mail system you have established connectivity with. Link Monitors do this by periodically sending messages to the specified servers or foreign mail systems and looking at the reply or NDR generated and the round-trip time taken to determine if the messaging link is functioning. If something is wrong with the link, appropriate actions can be taken, such as generating a Windows NT administrative alert, sending an email notification to an administrator, restarting services, or even rebooting the server.

When you create a new Link Monitor, it is located in the Monitors container in your site Configuration container. When you create a Link Monitor object, here are some of the things you need to consider when configuring its property sheet (Fig. 12-4):

- *Polling Interval.* A polling interval specifies how frequently the Link Monitor sends an email message to check for messaging connectivity with the designated Exchange servers or foreign mail systems. Just as for Server Monitors described earlier, the General tab lets you specify two different polling intervals:

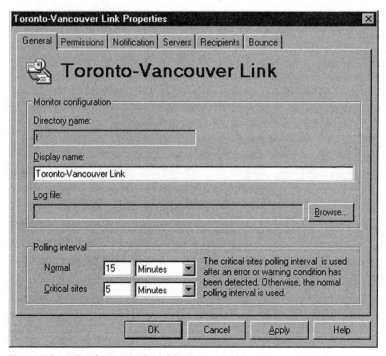

Figure 12-4   Configuring a Link Monitor.

- *Normal.*   This specifies how often the monitor sends messages over links that are running properly. The default is every 15 minutes.
- *Critical.*   This specifies how often the monitor sends messages over links that are detected as having a problem, such as when a LAN or WAN connection fails. The default is every 5 minutes.

- *Escalation Path.*   Just as for Server Monitors.

- *Servers.*   If you want to monitor the messaging links within your Exchange organization, select servers from your various sites to monitor here. For monitoring messaging links with foreign mail systems, see the next point.

- *Recipients.*   To monitor connectivity with foreign mail systems, you must first create a custom recipient that does not exist on the foreign mail system but that otherwise has the correct addressing information. For example, if you want to use a Link

Monitor to test connectivity with an Internet SMTP host called
mail.othercorp.com, you could create a custom recipient
called

```
bounce_me@mail.othercorp.com
```

This recipient should not exist on the foreign mail system.
When the Link Monitor sends a message to this address, the
foreign mail system should receive it, recognize that it is a
nonexistent recipient, and return a nondelivery report (NDR)
to the Link Monitor. The NDR then confirms that the link is
operational, if it is returned in the expected bounce time.

- *Bounce.* Here you specify what round-trip (bounce) times will
  be considered acceptable and what times will cause the link to
  be considered in an alert or warning state. These settings are
  used only if you are monitoring links with foreign mail systems.

- *Log File.*   You can have the monitor create an additional log file
  recording the status of the links being monitored. Use the General tab to configure this option.

Once you configure your new Link Monitor (and you can create several of them if you want to), you need to start it. Just as for
Server Monitors, you can start a Link Monitor two ways: manually or automatically. Starting a Link Monitor opens the Link
Monitor's status window (Fig. 12-5), allowing you to immediately
see the status of your messaging links using the symbols in the
first column of the window.

If you observe in the monitor's status window that a monitored
link is in a problem state, you can double-click on the link to
open a property sheet that gives more information about the
problem. For the selected link, this property sheet displays

- The time when the last message was sent over the link and
  when the bounced message was received, as well as any pend-
  ing request messages that have been sent but have not yet
  bounced

- What notifications have already been sent automatically concerning the problem

- The maintenance status of the monitored server

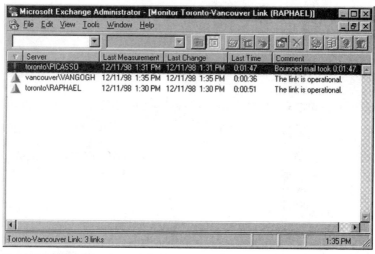

Figure 12-5   The status window for a Link Monitor that is running.

Message Queues

If users report problems with email not being delivered, another thing you can check is the various Exchange message queues. Exchange maintains a number of message queues for the Message Transfer Agent (MTA) and installed connectors such as the Internet Mail Service or MS Mail Connector. If one of these queues contains a lot of messages waiting to be delivered, it could indicate a connection problem, a configuration problem, or some other problem. If a corrupt message is stuck at the top of a queue and blocking other messages, you can delete the problem message or, in some queues, rearrange the order in which the queued messages will be processed. You also can check the Windows NT application log concerning problems associated with message queues.

To view the message queue for the MTA or some connector, open the object's property sheet and select the Queues tab on that property sheet. Figure 12-6 shows the Queues tab of the Message Transfer Agent property sheet for server Raphael in site Toronto. Notice that there is a messaging waiting in the MTA queue that handles messages being routed to the server Vangogh in the site Vancouver. This message is from user Admin4 and has the size and submission time shown in the figure.

Figure 12-6 Looking at what's in the MTA queue for messages outbound to server Vangogh.

By selecting the message and clicking the Details button, we can see more detailed information, including the full distinguished name of the sender, the unique ID number of the message, and the priority (Fig. 12-7). By using the other buttons, we can change the priority of the message, delete it from the queue, or refresh the view of the queue.

NOTE
More details are available for queued messages when you use the Queues tab on a connector's property sheet.

Performance Monitor

Finally, good-old Windows NT Performance Monitor is a useful tool for monitoring the health of your Exchange servers and mes-

Details   ☒

Originator:

DN:/o=SAMPLECORP/ou=TORONTO/cn=RECIPIENTS/cn=ADMIN4§C=US;A=
;P=samplecorp;O=toronto;S=4;G=admin;

MTSID: C=US;A= ;P=samplecorp;L=RAPHAEL-981211195230Z-11

Submit time: 12/11/98 1:52 PM   Priority: Normal   Size: 41

Close   Help

Figure 12-7   The details of the queued message from the preceding figure.

saging connections. We won't go into detail of how Performance
Monitor works or what Performance Monitor counters should be
used to monitor basic Windows NT Server memory, disk, network, and processor subsystems. These are discussed in the book
in this series covering the Windows NT Enterprise exam. Instead,
we'll just summarize below a few of the more useful counters (out
of the hundreds available) that are specific to Exchange and can
be used to monitor different Exchange components and services.

TIP
If you get a Performance Monitor-related problem that
deals with basic disk, memory, processor, and network subsystem performance issues, the correct solution probably will be
"Add more RAM!"

Directory Service

MSExchangeDS:Pending Replication Synchronzation.   This becomes
zero when all servers in your organization have responded to a
directory replication request. If this doesn't ever reach zero, you
may have connectivity problems with some servers in your
organization.

MSExchangeDS:Remaining Replication Updates.   This becomes zero
when your server has processed all directory replication
updates it has received. If this never becomes zero, directory
replication may not be completing before the next replication
cycle is initiated.

Private Information Store

MSExchangeIS Private:Average Time for Local Delivery. This indicates how long messages sent to other recipients on the same server wait in the Information Store queue before being delivered. If this is high, you may have problems with your Information Store.

MSExchangeIS Private:Average Time for Delivery. This indicates how long messages sent to recipients on other servers wait in the Information Store queue before being delivered. If this is high, you may have problems with your MTA.

Message Transfer Agent

MSExchangeMTA:Messages/Sec. This indicates messaging traffic (number of messages your server's MTA sends and receives each second).

MSExchangeMTA:Work Queue Size. This indicates how many messages are waiting in the MTA queues (inbound and outbound). If this is high, you may have a server performance problem—beef it up!

MSExchangeMTA Connections:Queue Length. This lets you examine the MTA queue for individual connections (instances) to see which connection, if any, is causing problems.

Where Do We Go from Here?

In the next chapter we will look at how we can *maintain* an Exchange organization by using log files, messaging tracking, and database maintenance utilities, performing backups, and using the Exchange Performance Optimizer.

For Review

1. What is a Server Monitor used for?
2. What is the polling interval for a monitor?
3. Explain what an *escalation path* is, and give an example.
4. State the three kinds of escalation notifications that a monitor can generate.
5. What is the difference between an Alert state and a Warning state? What symbols represent these states?

6. What three actions can Server Monitors perform on a stopped Windows NT service?

7. How can you synchronize the clocks of several different Exchange servers with your server?

8. How do you manually start a monitor?

9. How can you automatically start a monitor?

10. What does it mean to put an Exchange server into maintenance mode? How do you do it?

11. What can a Link Monitor be used for (two things)?

12. How do you configure a Link Monitor to check messaging with other servers in your organization?

13. How do you configure a Link Monitor to check messaging with a foreign mail system you have set up a connector for?

14. What kind of recipient do you need to create to test messaging connectivity with a foreign mail system?

15. What is *bounce time?*

16. What are *message queues,* and how can you view them?

17. What can you do with a corrupt message that is blocking a queue?

18. What are some common Exchange counters you might want to measure using Windows NT Performance Monitor?

CHAPTER 13

Maintenance

This chapter looks at tools and practices for maintaining a Microsoft Exchange-based organization. Topics covered include

- Database and log files
- Database maintenance
- Performing backups
- Performance Optimizer
- Troubleshooting tools
- Where do we go from here?
- For review

Database and Log Files

Exchange stores its directory and information store data in a series of databases. These databases are based on Microsoft's Joint Engine Technology (JET) database technology, an advanced 32-bit multithreaded transaction-based database technology. The size of the database files is unlimited in the Enterprise edition of Microsoft Exchange Server 5.5, although from the standpoint of current hardware technology the maximum size is 16 terabytes (1 terabyte = 1024 gigabytes).

■ The *directory database* consists of a database file DIR.EDB and its associated transaction log file plus other related files. The directory database maintains all Exchange directory information such as recipient properties and component configurations and is replicated to all Exchange servers in an organization. The directory database is maintained by the Exchange Directory Service, a Windows NT service running on Exchange servers.

■ The *information store* consists of two database files, one for the private information store (PRIV.EDB) and one for the public information store (PUB.EDB), plus the associated transaction logs file and other related files. The *private information store database* maintains all messages and attachments for those users whose home server is the specified Exchange server. The *public information store database* maintains all public folder contents for those public folder replicas hosted on the specified Exchange server. Both information store databases are maintained by the Exchange Information Store Service, a Windows NT service running on Exchange servers.

The critical database files and their associated transaction logs are listed in Table 13-1.

Transaction Logs

The transaction log file associated with each Exchange database performs the important function of helping to maintain the consistency and accuracy of the database files. To see how transaction logs work, let's take the directory database DIR.EDB as an example. When information needs to be written to or modified in the directory database file DIR.EDB, the Exchange Directory Service instead writes the information sequentially (one record at a time) to the associated transaction log file EDB.LOG as a series of transactions. After a short delay, these uncommitted transactions are committed; that is, they are written to the directory database file and marked in the log file as having been committed. Because of this delay, you should never consider any of the Exchange database files (*.EDB files) as being 100 percent up to date and accurate unless you also consider the uncommitted transactions in the associated transaction logs.

Table 13-1 Exchange Database Files and Transaction Logs

Component	File	Default Path
Information store	Private information store database	`\exchsrvr\mdbdata\PRIV.EDB`
	Public information store database	`\exchsrvr\mdbdata\PUB.EDB`
	Transaction log	`\exchsrvr\mdbdata\EDB.LOG`
Directory	Directory database	`\exchsrvr\dsadata\DIR.EDB`
	Transaction log	`\exchsrvr\dsadata\EDB.LOG`

The purpose of the transaction logs is two-fold:

- To improve server write performance using fast-written write-ahead files
- To provide fault-tolerance for the Exchange databases

The way it works is that when data is written to a transaction log, it is written simultaneously to a cache in memory. The information in this cache is later written to the database files, and once this is done, the associated transactions in the transaction log are marked as committed. If the server crashes before the cached information can be written to the database, Exchange can reconstruct the cached information on restart using the transaction log, since the lost cached information consists of all transactions in the log that are not yet marked as committed. Moreover, if the database files somehow become corrupted on the hard drive, Exchange can use the transaction logs to try to reconstruct the lost information, provided there is a complete set of transaction logs available from the time of the last backup.

Exchange log files normally accumulate sequentially until you

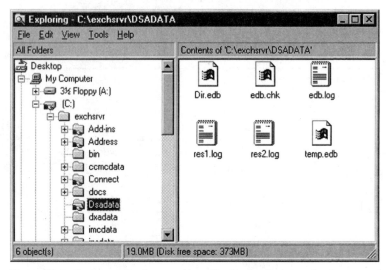

Figure 13-1   Exchange database and log files for the directory database.

perform a full or incremental backup, at which time all log files that contain only committed transactions are deleted, because they are no longer necessary. If you perform a differential backup, these log files are backed up but are still left on the hard disk too.

There are actually several kinds of log files used by Exchange to maintain the Exchange database files. These files are shown in Figure 13-1 and described in Table 13-2.

Transaction log files are always exactly 5 MB in size and have the name EDB.LOG. When a transaction log is filled by having all its transactions committed, it becomes a Previous Log file and is then renamed EDBxxxxx.LOG, where xxxxx is some number, and a new EDB.LOG file is created.

Circular Logging

Circular logging is a feature that enables the recycling of transaction log files by overwriting transaction logs that have already had all their data committed to the database. When you enable circular logging, you prevent the buildup of previous logs and thus conserve disk space. If you disable circular logging, old transaction logs, when committed, are saved as previous logs, which can use up a lot of disk space.

By default, circular logging is turned on for Microsoft Exchange

Table 13-2 Exchange Log Files that Help Maintain the Database Files

Type of File	File Name	Description
Transaction logs	EDB.LOG	These files temporarily store information before writing it to the database files. The information store and directory can have only one current transaction log at a given time.
Previous logs	EDBxxxxx.LOG	These are transaction logs that have had all their transactions committed. These files are maintained only if circular logging is disabled.
Checkpoint files	EDB.CHK	These files track which transactions in the transaction log have already been committed. When a transaction is committed, the checkpoint advances.
Reserved logs	RES1.LOG, RES2.LOG	These logs are used for emergency situations such as low disk space to ensure that no transactions are lost.
Temporary files	TMP.EDB	These files temporarily store transactions in progress and are used for transient storage during on-line compaction.
Patch files	*.PAT	These are temporary log files used during on-line backups.

servers. To turn it off, use the Advanced tab of the specified Server object's property sheet (Fig. 13-2).

Circular logging can substantially reduce the amount of disk space needed for your Exchange server to operate, but enabling circular logging has some disadvantages as well:

■ You can't perform incremental or differential backups of your Exchange server. This is so because these types of backups rely

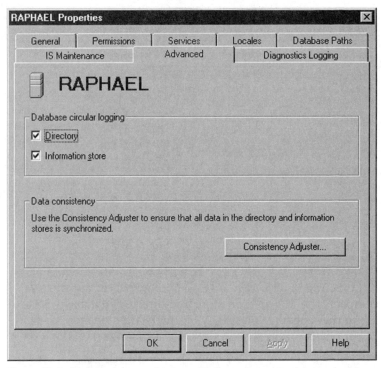

Figure 13-2 Use the Advanced tab on the Server property sheet to enable or disable circular logging on each database for a specific Exchange server.

on the presence of old transaction logs (previous logs) to be able to work properly. You can only perform full (normal) backups when circular logging is turned on.

- If your hard disk crashes, you can only restore the database files to the last full backup, not to the last transaction. This means that some information can be lost, so don't enable circular logging if data recoverability is a high priority for your organization.

You probably will want to turn circular logging off and make sure you have enough disk space to accommodate the accumulating log files. After all, additional disk drives are quite cheap these days. The only time you might want to turn circular logging on is for dedicated servers that host noncritical data such as a dedicated Exchange NNTP server.

NOTE

If Exchange is installed on a server with more than one hard drive (recommended), the log files described earlier are created on a separate disk from the database files. This is recommended to increase the chances of recovering the system successfully from a drive failure. Since log files are written rapidly and sequentially, the best type of disk configuration for locating the log files is a stripe set.

You can modify the location of the Exchange database and log files manually using the Database Paths tab of the Server object's property sheet for your Exchange server.

Database Maintenance

Databases can become fragmented over time, and thus they need to be defragmented regularly. Exchange Server automatically compacts the information store and directory databases according to the schedule you specify on the IS Maintenance tab of the Server object's property sheet for each Exchange server, but there may be times when you want to perform this action manually.

NOTE

It is best to perform your daily backups *after* the scheduled information store maintenance takes place on your Exchange servers.

Here are three command-line utilities that can be used by administrators for maintaining the Exchange Server database files.

ESEUTIL

This utility can be used to check the consistency of the information store and directory databases at the JET level of operation. ESEUTIL can be used to defragment these two databases, especially the information store databases, which shrink in size when they are defragmented (simply having users delete messages from their mailboxes has no effect on the size of the information store database files). ESEUTIL also can be used to check database consistency and attempt a recovery if your database becomes corrupted and you cannot restore it from backup.

ISINTEG

This utility can be used to check the consistency of the information store database files at the level of message storage. You must stop the Exchange Information Store service prior to running this utility. If you run ISINTEG with the -fix switch, it will try to fix any problems it finds in the database files. Microsoft recommends that you only use this utility under the direction of Microsoft Technical Support and that you back up the information store prior to running the utility.

MTACHECK

This utility can be used to check data stored by the Message Transfer Agent (MTA) in its *.DAT files. You must stop the Exchange Message Transfer Agent Service prior to running this utility. MTACHECK looks for messages that are damaged and are interfering with the processing of the message queues. If your Exchange Message Transfer Agent Service stops and you cannot start it using the Services utility in Control Panel, you can try running MTACHECK.

 NOTE
Of these three utilities, ESEUTIL is the most important. You may want to create a batch file that stops all Exchange services on your server, compacts the Exchange databases using ESEUTIL, and then restarts the Exchange services. You can then schedule this batch file to run once a week using the Windows NT at command.

Performing Backups

When you install Exchange Server on a Windows NT Server machine, the Windows NT Backup administrative tool is updated to allow simple on-line backup and restore of critical Exchange Server files (Fig. 13-3). For each Exchange server you back up, there will be two backup sets, one for the directory database and

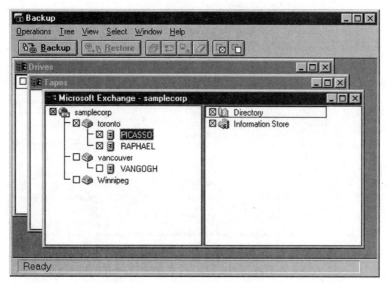

Figure 13-3   Backing up the Exchange Server database files using the enhanced Windows NT Backup utility.

one for the information store. Backing up the information store backs up the files in the \exchsrvr\mdbdata directory, whereas backing up the directory backs up files in the \exchsrvr\dsadata directory.

The actual files in these directories that are backed up depend on the type of backup performed:

- A full (normal) or copy backup will back up the *.EDB files.

- An incremental or differential backup will back up the *.LOG files.

You can schedule the Windows NT Backup utility by creating a batch file to run it from the command line and then use the Windows NT at command to schedule the batch file. The /is and /ds switches can be used with backup.exe to back up the information store and directory services databases.

Hardware Upgrades

If you need to upgrade your server's disk subsystem hardware, you will need to perform a full backup first. The restore process will then be as follows:

1. Reinstall Windows NT Server on the machine along with any Service Packs. Use the same organization, site, and computer names you used before. Use the same service account also.

2. Restore the directory, information store, and transaction logs from your backup tape.

3. Reboot the server and let it synchronize with other servers in your site.

NOTE
Be sure you understand the impact on the backup process of enabling or disabling circular logging on your Exchange server. Circular logging was discussed earlier in this chapter.

Performance Optimizer

When you first install Exchange Server on a machine, at the end of setup you are prompted to run the Performance Optimizer utility (`perfwiz.exe`). Performance Optimizer looks at the intended role of your server in the organization, analyzes your machine's hard disk subsystem, and suggests where various Exchange Server files should be located.

You should run Performance Optimizer again whenever you

- Add or remove hard disks
- Add another CPU
- Add more RAM
- Add or remove a connector or gateway
- Change the server's role, for example, making it a dedicated public folder server
- Change the server's expected load, for example, if you formerly optimized it for 500 users but now you expect to add another 500 more

Performance Optimizer runs as a Wizard that begins by stopping all Exchange services on the machine. The next screen of the Wizard asks for input regarding the role, configuration, and expected load of the server (Fig. 13-4). The settings you can select on this screen are as follows:

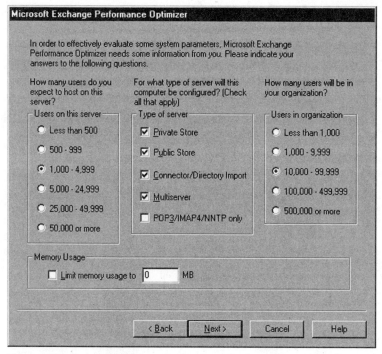

Figure 13-4 Running Exchange Performance Optimizer.

- Specify the number of mailboxes that will be homed on this server.

- Specify the total number of mailboxes in the entire organization.

- Specify the intended role(s) of the server by clearing or selecting checkboxes, specifically:

  - *Private Store* indicates that it will host mailboxes.
  - *Public Store* indicates that it will host public folder replicas.
  - *Connector/Directory Import* indicates that the server is used as a backbone or bridgehead server for connecting sites together or for establishing connectivity with foreign mail systems. It also indicates that the server may be used for bulk import or export of directory information, as during a migration.
  - *Multiserver* indicates there are other Exchange servers in the organization. Only clear this option if you are running a single Exchange server for your company.
  - *IMAP4/POP3/NNTP Only* indicates that the server is being

used for Internet mail and news only. Don't select this option if you are using MAPI clients such as Microsoft Outlook.

- By default, Exchange uses all available memory on the server. If you have another application running on the server, you can limit the amount of memory used by Exchange by using the setting at the bottom of this screen.

After completing the Wizard, Exchange services are restarted, and the results of running Performance Optimizer are saved in the log file:

```
C:\winnt\system32\perfopt.log
```

NOTE

If you run Performance Optimizer in verbose mode by typing `perfwiz -v` at the command prompt, you will have six additional dialog boxes to play with. This is for advanced users only.

Troubleshooting Tools

There are some additional tools that administrators can use to troubleshoot and perform maintenance on Exchange servers. These are discussed briefly here.

RPC Ping

This utility on the Exchange compact disk can be used to verify that there is RPC connectivity between two servers on your network. Remember that Exchange servers in the same site must be able to communicate with each other using RPCs.

Inbox Repair Tool

This utility (`scanpst.exe`) can be used to fix problems with personal folders (`*.pst`) and off-line storage (`*.ost`) files, which were discussed in Chapter 9.

Message Tracking

Exchange allows administrators to track messages as they flow between various components on Exchange servers in the organi-

zation. This lets administrators locate a specific message, find slow or failed connectors, determine messaging delays over specified routes, or track and delete "spam" and other unauthorized messages.
To track messages on Exchange, you first need to enable message tracking. Message tracking can be enabled on four different Exchange components:

- *Information Store Site Configuration (General tab).* This enables message tracking for messages handled by the information store.

- *MTA Site Configuration (General tab).* This enables message tracking for messages handled by the message transfer agent (MTA).

- *Internet Mail Service (Internet Mail tab).* This enables message tracking for messages handled by the Internet Mail Service.

- *Microsoft Mail Connector (Interchange tab).* This enables message tracking for messages handled by the Microsoft Mail Connector.

When you enable message tracking on one of these components, the Exchange System Attendant Service records all activity for that component in a log file. These tracking logs are saved with the name yyyymmdd.log and are located in the directory

```
\exchsrvr\tracking.log
```

To analyze these logs, you can open the Message Tracking Center window using the Tools menu on the Exchange Administrator window. When you first start the Message Tracking Center, the Select Message to Track dialog box appears. Specify who sent the messages you want to track, who they were sent to, and the number of days to look back in the log files for the messages, and then click Find Now. Exchange will search the message tracking logs and display all messages matching your criteria (Fig. 13-5). You can click the Properties button to find out more details about any of the messages listed.
Once you have selected a particular message from the Select Message to Track dialog box and clicked OK, you are presented with the main Message Tracking Center window. Click the Track button to start tracking your message through the various Exchange components in your organization (Fig. 13-6).
To select another message to track, click Search. To find a message based on its message ID, or to search for messages from recip-

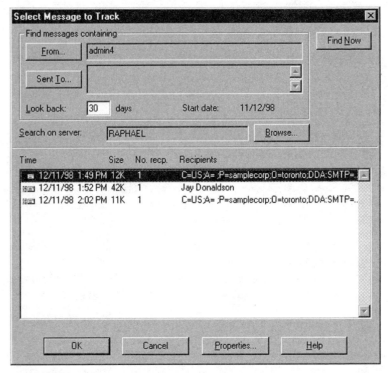

Figure 13-5   Selecting a message to track.

ients outside your organization, or to search for messages sent by Exchange services to each other, click Advanced Search.

Where Do We Go from Here?

In the final chapter we will look at a variety of *miscellaneous topics* that may be of importance to the exam but are not covered elsewhere in this book.

For Review

1. What are the file names for the directory and information store database files? Where are they located?

2. What are *transaction logs?* Why are they used with Exchange?

3. Describe the process by which transactions are written and then committed.

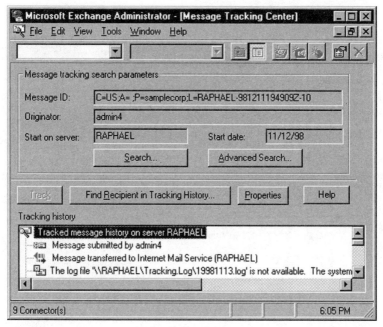

Figure 13-6 The Message Tracking Center window.

4. List the various log files and associate files and their functions.

5. When would you enable circular logging? What are the implications of doing this?

6. When would you disable circular logging? What are the implications of doing this?

7. How do you enable circular logging?

8. How can you manually change the location of the log files associated with Exchange databases?

9. How do you schedule automatic maintenance of the information store database?

10. What are each of the following utilities used for?

   - ESEUTIL
   - ISINTEG
   - MTACHECK

11. How does installing Exchange on a Windows NT Server modify the Windows NT Backup program?

12. What database files are backed up when a full or copy backup is performed?

13. What database files are backed up when an incremental or differential backup is performed?

14. How do you upgrade the disk subsystem for an Exchange server?

15. How does enabling or disabling circular logging affect your backup plan?

16. When should you run Performance Optimizer? What does it do?

17. What information do you have to provide for the Performance Optimizer Wizard?

18. Where does Performance Optimizer save its logged results?

19. What is RPC ping used for?

20. What is the Inbox Repair Tool used for?

21. How can you track messages through your Exchange organization?

22. What four components of Exchange can you enable message tracking on?

23. Where are message tracking logs saved?

24. What attributes of messages can you use when searching for a particular message to track?

CHAPTER 14

Miscellaneous

This chapter looks at a variety of Exchange topics not dealt with elsewhere in this book. Topics covered include

- Migration
- Export/import
- Domain mapping
- Chat Service
- Cluster Server
- Where do we go from here?
- For review

Migration

Migration essentially means moving users from one system to another. Microsoft Exchange includes a number of tools that make it easy for administrators to move users from other mail systems to Exchange. These tools enable administrators to copy mailbox properties and contents, distribution lists, address lists, and public folders from other mail systems to Exchange. Mail systems that can be migrated include certain versions of

- Microsoft Mail 3.x (PC and AppleTalk)
- Lotus cc:Mail versions DB6 and DB8
- Novell GroupWise 4.1
- Collabra Share
- IBM PROFS
- Vermation MEMO MVS
- Digital ALL-IN-1

This section briefly covers some of these migration tools and gives some insight into their use.

> **NOTE**
>
> Migration is usually performed in a series of steps, often weeks or months apart. As each step is completed, tests must be performed to ensure that users still have all the messaging capability they are used to. During migration, it is not unusual to have two or more mail systems running together, the new Exchange system and the older legacy systems or third-party systems. You must, of course, install the appropriate connectors on Exchange to allow messaging between your Exchange organization and the other mail systems during the migration period.

Migration Wizard

The Microsoft Exchange Migration Wizard (`mailmig.exe`) is a tool accessed from the Start menu that can assist administrators in migrating other mail systems to Exchange (Fig. 14-1). The Migration Wizard can be used to

- *Import from migration files.* This takes the migration files generated by a source extractor and imports this information into Microsoft Exchange.
- *Migrate from MS Mail for PC Networks to Exchange.* This gives the option either of migrating information directly from a Microsoft Mail system into Exchange or of extracting a user list from the MS Mail Postoffice in the form of a comma-delimited

Figure 14-1   The Exchange Migration Wizard.

(*.CSV) text file. This user list can then be edited if desired and imported into Exchange by running the Migration Wizard a second time and selecting Migrate from MS Mail for PC Networks again.

- *Migrate from Lotus cc:Mail to Exchange.* This gives the option either of migrating information directly from a Lotus cc:Mail system into Exchange or of using a source extractor to generate a series of migration files. These migration files can then be edited if desired and imported into Exchange by running the Migration Wizard a second time and selecting Import from Migration Files.

- *Migrate from Novell GroupWise to Exchange.* This gives the option either of migrating information directly from a Novell GroupWise mail system into Exchange or of using a source extractor to generate a series of migration files. These migration files can then be edited if desired and imported into Exchange by running the Migration Wizard a second time and selecting Import from Migration Files.

- *Migrate from Collabra Share to Exchange.* This gives the option either of migrating information directly from a Collabra Share mail system into Exchange or of using a source extractor to generate a series of migration files. These migration files can then be edited if desired and imported into Exchange by running the Migration Wizard a second time and selecting Import from Migration Files.

The *source extractors* for the cc:Mail, GroupWise, and Collabra Share migrations described earlier are tools that extract directory and recipient information from a mail system and copy this information to a series of *migration files*. These migration files can then be edited manually if desired and imported into Exchange using the Migration Wizard's first option, Import from Migration Files. The migration files generated by a source extractor include:

- *A Packing List file.* This file lists the primary and secondary migration files and specifies the code page for the files (for international use). The packing list file is a text file that has a *.PKL extension, but it stores information in a comma-delimited *.CSV format.

- *Primary files.* These contain directory information (recipient attributes such as address and phone number), message headers, personal address book and distribution lists entries, and pointers to secondary files. The primary files have a *.PRI extension, but they store the information in a comma-delimited *.CSV format.

- *Secondary files.* These contain actual data such as message bodies, attachments, and schedule information. The secondary files have a *.SEC extension and store information in both comma-delimited and raw binary format.

Import from Migration Files

If a source extractor has been used to generate a series of migration files, the Migration Wizard can then be used to import these files into Exchange using the Import from Migration Files option (see Fig. 14-1). Migration files are imported the same way regardless of the kind of mail system they came from. The Migration Wizard should be run on the Exchange server to which you want to import the files, and the migration files themselves should be moved to the hard drive on your target Exchange server prior to running the Wizard. These steps will ensure best performance during migration.

The steps involved in importing migration files are

1. Select Import from Migration Files in the Migration Wizard.
2. Specify the path to the Packing List File (*.PKL).
3. Specify the destination Exchange server.
4. Select the destination Recipients container.
5. Specify a template recipient (optional).
6. Indicate rules for generating new Windows NT accounts.
7. Start the migration process.

> **NOTE**
> Any restrictions you place on the template recipient, such as limiting the information store storage limit to a certain number of megabytes, will be applied during the migration process.

Migrate from MS Mail for PC Networks

The steps involved in migrating information *directly* from an existing mail system into Exchange depend on the type of mail system from which you are migrating. As an example, the steps involved in migrating information directly from a Microsoft Mail 3.x network into Exchange are

1. Select Migrate from MS Mail for PC Networks in the Migration Wizard.
2. Specify the path to the MS Mail Postoffice and the MS Mail administrator account.
3. Select One-Step Migration and Migrate to a Microsoft Exchange Computer.
4. Select what information you want to import: mailboxes, messages, shared folders, personal address books, schedule information.
5. Specify which MS Mail mailboxes you want to import.
6. Specify the name of the Exchange server to which you want to import the information and the Recipients container on this server into which to import the information.

7. Specify a mailbox template account if desired.

8. Indicate rules for generating new Windows NT accounts.

9. Start the migration process.

Export/import

The Directory Export and Directory Import options available under the Tools menu of the Exchange Administrator program have two functions:

- If you cannot do a migration from another mail system using the Migration Wizard, you can use the Directory Import command to import mailboxes from the other mail system, provided you are able to export this information from the other mail system into a properly formatted *.CSV file. Note that you can use this tool to import mailbox properties but not mailbox contents (i.e., messages and attachments).

- You can use Directory Export to export the properties (directory attributes) of a subset of your Exchange recipients to a *.CSV text file. You can then open this text file using a text editor, spreadsheet program, or database program and make whatever changes you want to the file. Finally, you can use Directory Import to import these changes back into your Exchange directory database. In other words, using this procedure, you can make modifications to the properties of lots of mailboxes all at once. For example, you might use this technique to change the style of display names of mailboxes, custom recipients, and distribution lists; change the format of email addresses; change everyone's telephone prefix; change the home server (and thus move the recipients to another Exchange server); and so on.

Directory Export

Figure 14-2 shows the Directory Export dialog box, opened using the Tools menu in the Exchange Administrator program. You can use this utility to export directory information for Exchange mailboxes, custom recipients, and distribution lists in your site. If you create a *new* *.CSV file using this tool, the resulting file will have the following header:

```
Obj-Class,First Name,Last name,Display Name,Alias Name,Direc-
tory Name,Primary Windows NT Account,Home-Server,E-mail
address,E-mail Addresses,Members,Obj-Container,Hide from AB
```

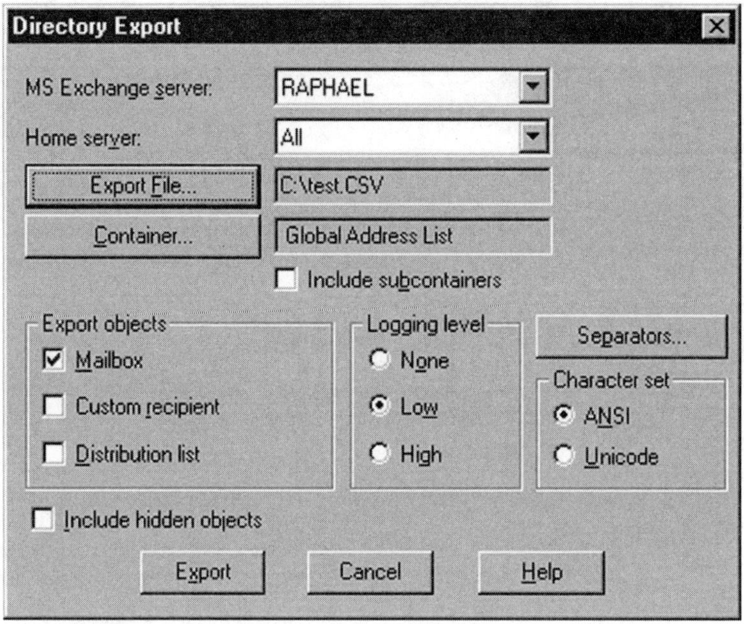

Figure 14-2 Using the Directory Export utility.

Each field in the preceding header represents an Exchange directory *schema attribute*. Table 14-1 explains the various fields in this header.

Alternatively, instead of exporting to a new *.CSV file, you can create a *.CSV file ahead of time with a header consisting of the particular schema attributes *you* want to export. For example, you might include a field for Phone Number or some other recipient attribute.

Using the Directory Export dialog box is simple enough. Just specify

- The Exchange server whose directory will be used to supply the required information

- The home server(s) that have the recipients you want to export

- The name of the export *.CSV file

- The container whose recipients will be exported and whether to export from subcontainers also

- The type(s) of recipients to be exported: mailboxes, custom recipients, and/or distribution lists

Table 14-1   Understanding Directory Export `*.CSV` files.

Schema Attribute	Meaning	Example
Obj-Class	Type of recipient	`Mailbox`
First Name	First name	`John`
Last Name	Last name	`Dough`
Display Name	Display name	`John Dough`
Alias Name	Alias name	`JohnD`
Directory Name	Internal directory name of recipient	`JohnD`
Primary Windows NT Account	Primary Windows NT Account	`DOMAIN44\JohnD`
Home-Server	Home server	`PICASSO`
E-mail Address	Email address	(contains the email address for a custom recipient)
E-mail Addresses	A string enclosed with double quotes containing the various email addresses for the recipient, with the "%" sign as a separator between them	`SMTP:JohnD@toronto.` `samplecorp.com%MS:` `SAMPLECORP/TORONTO/` `JOHND%X400:c=US;a=;` `p=samplecorp;` `o=toronto;s=Dough;` `=John;%CCMAIL:Dough,` `John at toronto`
Members	Distribution List members	(For distribution lists only)
Obj-Container	Parent Recipients container	`/ou=toronto/cn=` `Recipients`
Hide from AB	Whether recipient is hidden or not	0 (boolean)

- The even logging level for the export process
- The type of separator used in the *.CSV file
- Whether to include hidden recipients or not
- The character set used when creating the *.CSV file

Directory Import

Figure 14-3 shows the Directory Import utility. Import files are the same as export files, except that import files must contain a Mode file that specifies whether to update, create, modify, or delete the object in the Exchange directory. For example, the following *.CSV file was produced using Directory Export and had the

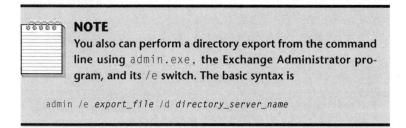

Figure 14-3 Using the Directory Import utility.

Mode property manually added for each recipient:

```
Obj-Class,Mode,First Name,Last name,Display Name...
Mailbox,create,Bob,Thomson,Bob Thomson,BobT...
Mailbox,modify,Don,Birkhoff,Don Birkhoff,DonB...
Mailbox,delete,Donna,Lepkie,Donna Lepkie,DonnaL...
```

> **NOTE**
>
> If you are going to modify recipient information in the Exchange directory using Directory Import, the records in the *.CSV file must contain entries for the following three attributes:
>
> - Obj-Class
> - Directory Name
> - Home-Server
>
> Without these three attributes, the directory import process can't associate the information with existing Microsoft Exchange accounts. If the program you exported the information from doesn't contain these three fields, you must manually create them in the *.CSV file.

Using the Directory Import dialog box is also straightforward. Just specify

- The Windows NT domain in which new user accounts will be created.
- The Exchange server into which you want to import the information.
- The container into which the recipients will be imported or whose recipients will be modified or deleted.
- The recipient template object.
- The path to the import *.CSV file. This file can be located anywhere on the network, as long as it is accessible. Best performance will be achieved, however, by first moving the import file to the target Exchange server.
- Rules for generating Windows NT accounts for new recipients or deleting accounts for deleted recipients.
- The even logging level for the export process.
- The type of separator used in the *.CSV file.

■ Whether to Append or Overwrite imported data in multivalued
attributes. You might use Append, for example, if you wanted
to use Directory Import to create an *additional* SMTP address for
every recipient in your site. Email Addresses is an example of a
multivalued attribute, since it can have more than one value.
Multivalued attributes are enclosed in double quotes with the
"%" sign separator between each value (see Table 14-1).

NOTE
You also can perform a directory import from the command
line using `admin.exe`, **the Exchange Administrator program, and its** `/i` **switch. The basic syntax is**

```
admin /i import_file /d directory_server_name
```

Domain Mapping

Domain mapping refers to how you map the topology of your
Exchange organization (its sites and how they are connected) to
the topology of your enterprise's Windows NT domains (its
domains and trust relationships). The important things to
remember are

■ All Exchange servers in the same site must use the same service
account.

■ Windows NT user accounts must either be in

  ■ The *same domain* as their Exchange server.
  ■ A domain that the Exchange server's domain trusts, that is, a
  trusted domain (Fig. 14-4).

NOTE
The same holds true if you want to administer an Exchange
server: Your Administrator account must either be in the
same domain as the Exchange server or in a trusted
domain. All the Exchange Administrator accounts in a trusted
domain can be grouped together into a Global Group to simplify
the assigning of permissions.

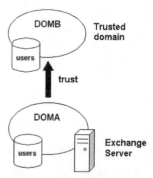

Figure 14-4 Exchange Server and Windows NT domains.

Chat Service

The Microsoft Exchange Chat Service enables real-time collaboration between users with any standard IRC or IRCX client. Using the Chat Service you can create chat rooms and grant different levels of access to different users. Levels of access are assigned to users globally for all chat channels. These access levels include

- *Hosts.* These users have full control over the chat room.
- *Participants.* These users can read and participate in discussions.
- *Spectators.* These users can read a discussion but can't participate in it.
- *Anonymous Access.* Optional.

A special Windows NT account called the *Chat User account* is used to grant permissions to users for accessing chat channels. If necessary, you can create additional chat accounts for a chat channel and use these accounts to provide different permissions to users of this particular channel. For example, if you want to allow some users access to most chat channels but deny them access to a specific channel #ManagerTalk, you can create an additional chat account for that channel and assign those users the permission NONE.

Cluster Server

Microsoft Cluster Server is included in Windows NT Server 4.0 Enterprise Edition and enables two NT servers to act together as a cluster. A *cluster* consists of two Windows NT Server computers that share a unique computer name and IP address. The two nodes (servers) in a cluster are physically connected using a common SCSI disk subsystem. This provides fail-over support for applications such as Exchange—if one node in the cluster crashes, the other one can take over running the application in a matter of seconds.

Microsoft Cluster Server enables Exchange implementations to provide 24 × 7 × 365 support for users (and 29 × 8 × 365 working hours for administrators—just kidding!)

Where Do We Go from Here?

That's it! If you've read through this book without doing any of the For Review questions, you should try these questions now, since they will test your knowledge and understanding of Exchange concepts and practices. If you can't answer a question, reread the section in the chapter dealing with that topic, and try again. Otherwise, it's time to try your luck with the exam.

Good luck!

For Review

1. What does *migration* mean?
2. What legacy and third-party mail systems can be migrated to Exchange?
3. What is the primary tool for migrating other mail systems to Exchange?
4. What do you need to install in your Exchange organization during the weeks or months in which your migration is being performed?
5. What are the five kinds of migration that can be performed using the Migration Wizard?
6. Why might you not perform a direct migration between your previous mail system and Exchange?
7. What is a *source extractor?* Name some source extractors included with Exchange. How do you run them?
8. What are the various migration files produced by a source extractor? What information is in each file?

9. Describe the steps involved in a typical MS Mail migration.

10. What two things can you do with the Directory Import/Export utilities?

11. Describe the format of the *.CSV file produced by Directory Export.

12. Why would you create your own header for a *.CSV file before performing Directory Export?

13. How can you run Directory Export from the command prompt?

14. What additional attribute must an import file have that an export file doesn't? Why?

15. What three attributes must be in an import file if you are making modifications to recipient attributes in your Exchange directory?

16. What is a *multivalued attribute?*

17. How can you run Directory Import from the command prompt?

18. What considerations are important when mapping your Exchange site topology to your Windows NT domain topology?

19. What kinds of access can you assign to chat rooms using the Exchange Chat Service?

20. Does Microsoft Exchange work with Microsoft Cluster Server?

Index

Active Server Pages (ASP), 58
Address book views, 145–152
    adding recipients to, 150
    creating, 145, 147–149
    definition of, 145
    examples of, 145–147
    moving recipients in, 152
    review questions, 152
    using, 150
Addresses:
    e-mail, 174–178
    site, 85–87
Admin.exe, 64
Affinity (public folders),
    138–140
Anonymous accounts, 80
Application Log, 65
ARPANET, 199
ASP (Active Server Pages), 58
Associations, 85
Attributes, 80–81
Aviation testing centers, 27

Backups, 244–246
Bandwidth, network, 53
Beta exams, 16–17
Bridgehead servers, 51, 54,
    89, 184

CALs (see Client access
    licenses)
CAs (Certificate Authorities),
    206
CAT exams (see Computer
    adaptive testing exams)

cc:Mail, 178, 195, 255
Certificate Authorities (CAs),
    206
Certification, MCSE (see
    MCSE certification)
Chat, 47
Chat Service, 264
Chat User account, 264
Cheat notes, 38
Checkpoint size, 84
Circular logging, 240–243
Client access licenses (CALs),
    56–57
Client permissions (see Per-
    missions)
Clients, 47–48, 153–171
    with Microsoft Internet
        Mail and News, 168
    with Microsoft Outlook,
        155–166
    with Microsoft Outlook
        Express, 167–168
    with Microsoft Outlook
        Web Access, 168–170
    with Microsoft Schedule+,
        166–167
    review questions, 170–171
Collabra Share, 255–256
Computer adaptive testing
    (CAT) exams, 34–35
Connectivity, 53–54
Connectors, 46, 51, 173–196
    and addressing, 174–178
    for cc:Mail, 195
    container for, 182

Connectors (*Cont.*):
definition of, 174
and directory synchronization, 190–195
Dynamic RAS Connector,
184–186
MS Mail Connector,
188–195
review questions,
195–196
and routing, 178–182
Site Connectors, 182–184
types of, 175
X.400 Connector, 186–188
Containers:
Configuration, 78–79
connector, 182
protocols, 207–208
server, 96–99
Contracts, 6–7
Core requirements (Microsoft
Windows NT 4.0 track), 2
Cost value (public folders),
138
CSV files, 258–262
Custom attributes, 80–81
Custom recipients, 50,
120–122

Daemons, 200
DDA (Domain Defined
Attribute), 181
Dedicated home servers, 54
Dedicated public folder
servers, 54
Delegate access (Microsoft
Outlook), 163–165
Dial-up networking (DUN),
184–186
Directory database (Exchange
Administrator), 65–66
Directory Export, 258–261

Directory Import, 258,
261–263
Directory replication, 50, 53,
87–89
Directory Service (DS),
101–103
Directory synchronization
(dirsync), 53, 88, 190–195
requestor, dirsync, 191–192
requestor, remote dirsync,
192
server, dirsync, 54–54, 192
Directory(-ies), 50
names of, 55–56
server-level, 93–96
site-level, 75–78
Distinguished names (DNs),
175–176, 178, 181
Distribution lists (DLs), 50,
54, 119–120
DNs (*see* Distinguished
names)
DNS (*see* Domain Name
System)
Domain Defined Attribute
(DDA), 181
Domain mapping, 263–264
Domain Name System (DNS),
177, 200
DS (*see* Directory Service)
DS Site Configuration, 79–81
DS/IS Consistency Adjuster
tool, 97–99
DUN (*see* Dial-up network-
ing)
Dynamic RAS Connector,
184–186

Edbutil.exe, 64
Elective requirements
(Microsoft Windows NT
4.0 track), 2–4

Escalation path, 224–225
ESEUTIL, 243–244
Exam Preparation Guide, 43
Exam(s):
  IIS 3.0, 14–15
  MCP, 8, 9, 17
  MCSE (*see* MCSE exams)
  PEP, 20–22
  TCP/IP, 14, 16
Exchange Administrator,
  63–74
  administrative tools
    included with, 63–65
  configuring options for, 70
  installing, 67–68
  permissions, 70–74
  review questions, 74
  user interface, 66–67
  using, 68–69
Exchange Service Account, 49
Exchange.prf, 160
Expansion servers, 54
Export, Directory, 258–261

Fault tolerance, 53–54
Feeds, 204, 218
Firewalls, 220–221
Folder Forms Library
  (Microsoft Outlook), 166
Foreign connectivity, 53
Forms (in Microsoft Out-
  look), 165–166

GALs (*see* Global address lists)
Garbage collection interval,
  80
Gateway Routing Table
  (GWART), 179–181
Gateways, 46, 51
Global address lists (GALs),
  47, 51, 113, 143–144,
  191–192

Global public folders,
  137–138
Graphic user interfaces
  (GUIs), 28
GWART (*see* Gateway Routing
  Table)

Hardware requirements:
  for Exchange Server, 57
  for MCSE exam, 5–6
  upgrades, 245–246
Hidden recipients, 112, 113
Hosts, 200
Hypertext Transfer Protocol
  (HTTP), 205

IIS (*see* Internet Information
  Server)
IIS 3.0 exam, 14–15
ILS (Internet Locator Server),
  47
IMAP4 (*see* Internet Mail
  Access Protocol version 4)
Import, Directory, 258,
  261–263
Inbound feeds, 218
Inbox Assistant (Microsoft
  Outlook), 165
Inbox Repair Tool, 248
Information Store Integrity
  Checker, 64
Information store (IS), 49, 97
Information Store Site Con-
  figuration, 81–82
Installation of Exchange
  Server, 57–59
International Telecommuni-
  cations Union (ITU), 176
Internet, 47, 199–222
  configuration of protocols
    for, 206–213
  DNS protocol, 200

Internet (*Cont.*):
  firewalls and security with, 220–221
  HTTP protocol, 205
  IMAP4 protocol, 202
  LDAP protocol, 205
  and MIME, 203–204
  NNTP protocol, 204
  origins of, 199
  POP3 protocol, 201–202
  review questions, 221–222
  and S/MIME, 204
  SMTP protocol, 200–201
  SSL protocol, 206
Internet Information Server (IIS), 58, 205
Internet Locator Server (ILS), 47
Internet Mail Access Protocol version 4 (IMAP4), 202, 210
Internet Mail Service, 211–217
Internet News Service, 204, 217–220
Internet Service Providers (ISPs), 212–213
IS (*see* Information store)
ISINTEG, 244
ISPs (*see* Internet Service Providers)
ITU (International Telecommunications Union), 176

Joint Engine Technology (JET), 237

Key Management (KM) server, 54, 58

LANs, 49, 53
Latency period, 99

LDAP (*see* Lightweight Directory Access Protocol)
Leaf objects, 96
Licensing, 56–57
Lightweight Directory Access Protocol (LDAP), 81, 205, 210, 211
Link Monitors, 51, 229–232
Locales, 96
Locations, user, 139–140
Log files:
  circular logging, 240–243
  transaction logs, 238–240

Mailbox agents, 50–51, 123
Mailboxes, 50, 115–119
  configuring, 116–118
  definition of, 115
  modifying, 119
  moving, 118
Maintenance, 237–252
  backups, 244–246
  and database files, 237–238
  of databases, 243–244
  and log files, 238–243
  with Performance Optimizer, 246–248
  review questions, 250–252
  tools for, 248–250
MAPI (*see* Messaging Application Programming Interface)
Mapping, domain, 263–264
"Mark" box (on MCSE exams), 41
MCIS (Microsoft Commercial Internet Server) Membership System, 203
MCP exams, 8, 9, 17
MCPs (*see* Microsoft Certified Professionals)

MCSE certification:
  costs of, 4–7
  myths about, 7–8, 10–12
  sources of information on,
    42
  time needed for, 10–11
  See also MCSE exams
MCSE exams:
  aviation testing centers
    for, 27
  beta exams, 16–17
  CAT exams, 34–35
  checking number/title of,
    40–41
  core vs. elective, 2–4
  exemptions from, 7–8
  exhibits on, 29
  indirect questions on,
    33–34
  marking questions on,
    41–42
  Networking Essentials
    exam, waiver of, 9
  nondisclosure agreement
    for, 39–40
  number of, 7–8
  old exams, retiring of,
    17–20
  optional online tutorial
    for, 39
  Personal Exam Prep
    exams, 20–22
  practice exams, 23–25
  preparing for, 22–23,
    25–26
  retaking, 11
  same-day testing, 26–27
  scenario questions on,
    30–32
  scheduling/rescheduling,
    27–28, 35–37
  sequence of, 12–15

MCSE exams (*Cont.*):
  simulation questions on,
    34
  strategies for taking, 29–34
  Sylvan interface for,
    32–33, 35–36
  testing centers for, 26, 27,
    37–38
  weekend testing, 26–27
MCSEs (Microsoft Certified
  Systems Engineers), 1
Message tracking, 248–250
Message Transfer Agents
  (MTAs), 49, 99–101, 189
  checking internal database
    of, 64, 244
  message queues for,
    232–233, 235
  routing by, 178–179
  Site Configuration object
    of, 83–85
Messaging Application Programming Interface
  (MAPI), 155–156
Microsoft Certificate Server,
  58
Microsoft Certified Profes-
  sionals (MCPs), 8–9
Microsoft Certified Systems
  Engineers (MCSEs), 1
Microsoft Cluster Server, 58,
  264–265
Microsoft Commercial Inter-
  net Server (MCIS) Mem-
  bership System, 203
Microsoft Exchange Server
  5.5, 45–61
  Chat service of, 47
  communication between
    clients and, 47–48
  configuration of, 59–60
  features of, 45–47

Microsoft Exchange Server
5.5 (*Cont.*):
functioning of, 47–48
installing, 57–59
interoperability of, 46
licensing issues, 56–57
migration to, 46–47
naming conventions with,
55–56
NetMeeting feature of, 47
permissions, 70–74
planning for implementa-
tion of, 51–56
reliability of, 47
security with, 47
terminology, 48–51
See also Exchange Administrator
Microsoft Internet Mail, 168
Microsoft Internet News,
168
Microsoft Mail Connector,
58, 188–195
Microsoft Outlook, 65,
143–144, 155–166
assistants in, 165
delegate access with,
163–165
forms in, 165–166
forms libraries in, 166
installing, 156–157
offline folders with,
161–162
Outlook Profile in,
157–161
remote mail with, 162–163
Microsoft Outlook Express,
167–168
Microsoft Outlook Web
Access, 168–170
Microsoft Schedule+,
166–167

Microsoft Windows NT, 2
administrative tools,
64–65
Microsoft Windows NT 4.0
track, 2–4
core requirements, 2
elective requirements, 2
Migration, 253–258
definition of, 253
Import from Migration
Files option, 256–257
from MS Mail for PC Net-
works, 257–258
tools for, 46–47
Wizard, Migration, 64,
254–256
MIME (*see* Multipurpose
Internet Mail Extensions)
Monitors/monitoring,
223–236
Link Monitors, 229–232
with message queues,
232–233
Performance Monitor,
233–235
review questions, 235–236
Server Monitors, 223–229
MS Mail for PC Networks,
254–255, 257–258
MTA Site Configuration,
83–85
MTACHECK, 244
mtacheck.exe, 64
MTAs (*see* Message Transfer
Agents)
Multipurpose Internet Mail
Extensions (MIME),
203–204

Naming conventions, 55–56
NDR (nondelivery report),
101

NetMeeting, 47
Network bandwidth, 53
Network News Transfer Protocol (NNTP), 204, 210, 211
Networking Essentials exam, waiver of, 9
Newsfeeds, 204, 218–220
Newsgroups, Microsoft, 42
NNTP (*see* Network News Transfer Protocol)
Nondelivery report (NDR), 101
Nondisclosure agreement, 39–40
None.prf, 160
Novell GroupWise, 255
NTLM (Windows NT Challenge/Response), 203

Offline address books, 80
Offline Folders (Microsoft Outlook), 161–162
Old exams, retiring of, 17–20
Operating systems (OS), 18
Organization Forms Library (Microsoft Outlook), 166
Organizations, 48
OS (operating systems), 18
Out of Office Assistant (Microsoft Outlook), 165
Outbound feeds, 218
Outlook Forms Designer, 166
Outlook.prf, 160

PEP exams (*see* Personal Exam Prep exams)
Performance Monitor, 65, 233–235
Performance Optimizer, 59, 64, 246–248

Permissions, 70–74, 80, 132–134
Personal Address Book (Microsoft Outlook), 159
Personal Exam Prep (PEP) exams, 20–22
Personal Folders (Microsoft Outlook), 159
Personal Forms Library (Microsoft Outlook), 166
Polling interval, 224, 229–230
Post Office Protocol version 3 (POP3), 201–202
Practice exams, 23–25
Private Information Store object, 103–105, 235, 238
Profgen.prf, 160–161
Public folders, 50, 127–141
  affinity, public folder, 138–140
  contents of, 128
  creating, 127–129
  definition of, 127
  global, 137–138
  as hidden objects, 128
  hierarchy of, 128, 134
  permissions for, 132–134
  properties of, 130–132
  replicas of, 134–138
  review questions, 140–141
Public Information Store object, 105–106, 135–137, 238
Pull feeds, 218
Push feeds, 218

Recipients, 50–51, 111–125, 230–231
  in address book views, 150, 152
  containers for, 112–114

Recipients (*Cont.*):
creating, 114–115
Custom Recipients, 120–122
definition of, 111
Distribution Lists, 119–120
hidden, 112, 113
Mailbox Agents, 123
mailboxes, 115–119
review questions, 124–125
template, 113–114
Recovery timeout, 84
Reliable Transfer Service (RTS), 84
Remote Mail (Microsoft Outlook), 162–163
Remote procedure calls (RPCs), 48, 49, 183
Replicas, public folder, 134–138
Rescheduling exams, 27–28
Retaking tests, 11
Rich Text Format (RTF), 203
Roadmap to Certification CD, 20
Roles (client permissions), 132–134
Routing, 178–182
to other sites/mail systems, 179–182
on same server, 178
within site, 178–179
RPC Ping, 248
RPCs (*see* Remote procedure calls)
RTF (Rich Text Format), 203
RTS (Reliable Transfer Service), 84

Saluki, 42
Same-day testing, 26–27
scanpst.exe, 248

Scenario questions (on MCSE exams), 30–32
Scheduling exams, 27–28, 35–37
Secure Multipurpose Internet Mail Extensions (S/MIME), 204
Secure Sockets Layer (SSL) protocol, 203, 206
Security, 47, 53, 220–221
Server Monitors, 51, 223–229
Server Recipients container, 112
Server(s), 49, 54–55, 93–109
directory objects, server-level, 93–96
and Directory Service object, 101–103
dirsync, 192
and MTAs, 99–101
and Private Information Store object, 103–105
and Public Information Store object, 105–106
review questions, 108–109
routing on same, 178
and server containers, 96–99
and System Attendant object, 106–108
Service accounts, 49–50
Shared-file mail systems, 48
Simple Mail Transfer Protocol (SMTP), 177, 200–201, 212–216
Simulation questions (on MCSE exams), 34
sinteg.exe, 64
Site Configuration container, 78–79
Site Connectors, 182–184

Site(s), 48–49, 52–54, 75–91
  addressing, 85–87
  Configuration container,
    78–79
  directory objects, site-
    level, 75–78
  directory replication,
    87–89
  DS Site Configuration,
    79–81
  Information Store Site
    Configuration, 81–82
  MTA Site Configuration,
    83–85
  review questions, 89–91
  routing within, 178–179
S/MIME (Secure Multipur-
  pose Internet Mail Extensions), 204
SMTP (see Simple Mail Transfer Protocol)
Software requirements:
  for Exchange Server, 57, 58
  for MCSE exam, 5
SSL protocol (see Secure Sockets Layer protocol)
Sylvan, 26, 28, 32–33, 35–36
System Attendant, 49,
  106–108

Target servers list, 183–184
TCP/IP exam, 14, 16
TechNet Trial CD, 22

Template recipients, 113–114
Testing centers, 26, 27,
  37–38
Tombstone markers, 80
Transaction logs, 238–240
Troubleshooting tools,
  248–250

Upgrades, hardware, 245–246
U.S. Department of Defense,
  199
USENET, 204, 218
User Manager for Domains,
  64–65

Virtual University Enterprises
  (VUE), 26–27, 35

WANs, 49, 53
Web browsers, 205
Web pages, 205
Web servers, 205
Weekend testing, 26–27
Windows Messaging Profiles
  (Microsoft Outlook),
  157–161
Windows NT
  Challenge/Response
  (NTLM), 203

X.400 Connector, 176–177,
  179, 186–188
X.500, 205

About the Author

Mitch Tulloch is a Microsoft Certified Trainer and MCSE who trains and consults for Productivity Point, Inc. He is the author of *Accelerated MCSE Study Guide: Internet Information Server 4.0* and *Administering IIS 4.0.*